'A delightful book – elegantly simple, insightful and inspiring.'

MARK WILLIAMSON
DIRECTOR OF ACTION FOR HAPPINESS

'A good strong voice...examining the role of meditation
in creating and maintaining greater happiness and
wellbeing in Western folk'

SUSAN CLARK
FORMERLY ASSOCIATE EDITOR OF *RESURGENCE & ECOLOGIST*

'The perfect beginner's handbook...beautifully designed'

EMMA THOMPSON
ACTRESS

Happiness and How It Happens

Finding Contentment Through Mindfulness

The Happy Buddha

Leaping Hare Press

This edition published in the UK and North America in 2016 by

Leaping Hare Press

Ovest House, 58 West Street
Brighton BN1 2RA, UK
www.quartoknows.com

First published in the UK in 2011

British Library Cataloguing-in-Publication Data
A catalogue record for this book is available from
the British Library

ISBN: 978-1-907332-93-7

This book was conceived, designed and produced by

Leaping Hare Press

Creative Director PETER BRIDGEWATER
Publisher SOPHIE COLLINS
Art Director WAYNE BLADES
Commissioning Editor MONICA PERDONI
Senior Editor JAYNE ANSELL
Designer RICHARD CONSTABLE
Illustrator SARAH YOUNG

Printed in China

1 3 5 7 9 10 8 6 4 2

CONTENTS

Introduction 6

CHAPTER ONE
Happiness 8

CHAPTER TWO
Starting Meditation 24

CHAPTER THREE
Accepting, Not Changing 50

CHAPTER FOUR
Meeting Your Emotions 76

CHAPTER FIVE
Waking Up 112

Afterword 139

Further Resources 140

Index 142

Dedication & Acknowledgements 144

INTRODUCTION

◆

This book is the fruit of my own exploration into that elusive quality we call happiness. It looks at what happiness (and also unhappiness) is and is not. Happiness and freedom may not be our present experience, but they can be — and it doesn't involve years and years of struggling with self-improvement.

T HE AIM OF THE BOOK is to show how, through mindfulness meditation and awareness practice, to work with our endlessly chattering minds, embrace difficult emotions such as fear and anger, and see through to our inherent loveliness and the happiness that awaits us. Most of all it shows that awareness is the secret to a life of happiness and freedom, which is available to everyone. You do not have to be a certain type of person to go on this journey, you don't have to be 'spiritual' or 'good' or have particular beliefs. You may have practised meditation in the past, or be completely new to it.

Is this Book for You?
The book is intended for you if you are looking for a way to discover the happiness and meaning you know lies within yourself. You may have been involved in conventional religion, or be on a spiritual path of self-improvement. It is for you if you do not want to take on a particular belief system or to live a proscribed life. It is for you if you sense that

happiness and freedom are achievable for all, irrespective of lifestyle and beliefs. It is for you if you sense that there is more to life than endlessly striving to better yourself and getting exhausted in the process. If you know there is more to life than amassing money and spending your way through it, then you will appreciate the message of this book.

Discovering Meditation

I first came across meditation in the early 1990s, and throughout my involvement in Buddhism, meditation has remained my main interest. It was in 2001 when I was living at Vajraloka, a meditation retreat centre in North Wales, that I realized that meditation was for everyone. I realized that while living a quiet life in a retreat centre was a valid way of living, meditation could be of immense value to all, irrespective of lifestyle. People come to my courses suffering the strains of modern-day life, and I see just how relevant meditation can be.

Meditation & Awareness Practice

In Chapter 2 you will learn how to practise mindfulness meditation. I suggest you keep to this as your daily meditation practice – follow the instructions and keep it simple. You will also come across awareness practices; here, I suggest you choose one or two at a time and explore them gradually.

CHAPTER ONE

HAPPINESS

*In order to understand how happiness happens,
we first need to understand what happiness is.
The good news, spiritual thinkers share, is that
happiness is our natural state of being, our true
nature — but most of us have lost touch with that,
and in the process of pursuing what we believe to
be happiness have somehow managed to make
ourselves unhappy. Our aim, therefore, is to
return to our natural state of happiness.*

PARADISE LOST – AND REGAINED

◆

Before we can be happy, we need to learn how we make ourselves unhappy, and as we see this – I mean really see it – we stop doing it to ourselves. It sounds simple, and it is, once you recognize what has brought you to your unnatural state of unhappiness.

WHEN WE ARE BORN, we live in a kind of paradise. Our desires are few and, if they are met quickly by our loving mother, we are content and happy. More significantly, we experience a state of blissful oneness with all life. As we grow up, we develop a sense of self as a distinct entity from all the other selves around us, and the paradise, the sense of oneness and connectedness with life – which at the time we didn't even know we had – is lost.

Searching for Paradise

What takes over is a firm and seemingly solid sense of *me* that believes it must battle against the world to get what it wants and needs. Our needs and wants become more complex and are no longer just about having food, shelter and warmth. To varying degrees we start to define our sense of worth as a person by what we own, and by our level of success in the world. This sense of self, though quite a natural part of growing up, nevertheless leaves us feeling separate from other people. It often leaves us in a state of 'quiet desperation'.

Each of us is looking to regain our paradise, and each of us, barring maybe a few exceptions, knows that *this*, my life as it is, certainly is not paradise. Of course we cannot go back to the state of blissful ignorance we had as a baby. But our hearts still yearn for this state of connectedness, for the happiness that the state of oneness gave us – so we search and search *outside* ourselves trying to find this lost state of contentment and happiness. But even if we have the 'good things' in life – lots of money, a loving partner, good friends – we see that it's not enough; we are still unfulfilled. We are still searching high and low for paradise in almost everything we do.

Spiritual Materialism

When we begin to see that paradise is not regained through acquiring more things, or more knowledge, or being important, or living a certain lifestyle, we may turn our attention to more spiritual matters. We may even start to meditate. Then we may think that paradise is to be found through meditation. Our attitude may be, 'Once I've calmed myself enough, or sorted myself out, nothing will bother me ever again.'

What happens is that our own personal (egoic) agenda for fixing the external world to be as we want it, which has never worked, gets shifted to the so-called spiritual world. Our attitude may be, 'If I cannot be happy by fixing the world as I want it to be, then I'll be happy by fixing myself, as I want to be.' This is called spiritual materialism – we come into the spiritual life because we want something out of it for ourselves. We take up meditation because we want to change ourselves into a different type of person. This, of course, is perfectly fine and may be a necessary phase to begin with. After all, if we're not going to get something out of practising meditation, then why bother doing it?

The Egoic Agenda

But to fulfil our own egoic agenda isn't the point of meditation. It's true that our life will change significantly for the better if we sit intelligently, but if we have our own agenda then we're going to be constantly disillusioned. The egoic agenda is always about how we will be in the future. Our agenda may be a desire to be a wiser person, or to be more compassionate – or even to be a great meditator.

The ego's only concern is its own survival, and that means looking to become something or somebody in the future; it means looking to an ideal it can transform itself into. But if we can come into our present experience, instead of moving towards an ideal, we will come to understand who we are, we will see through the illusion of the ego, and the question of being wiser or more compassionate will be irrelevant. Wisdom and compassion are there when the self, the ego, is acknowledged for what it is – an illusion. Wisdom doesn't belong to us, compassion doesn't belong to us; we could say they are impersonal.

Paradise Regained

The point of meditation is to bring light upon (enlighten) the egoic agenda, to become more aware of all our self-centred thinking and acting. The point of meditation, the point of awareness, is to die spiritually. This means that the self, which feels itself the centre of the universe, begins to wither and eventually die away, giving birth to our true nature. Our true nature is one of wisdom, openness, sensitivity to life and compassion for all.

Being here and now, with life simply as it is, is the paradise we have been seeking. It is the awakened state itself. The Buddha, the 'happy one', was happy because he was with life as it was happening, because he didn't get lost in opinions and judgements about how it should be different. It's not that he didn't experience pain. He did – but he didn't create suffering out of it. He didn't create the story of 'this pain is happening to poor old me'. There was pain, but nobody – no individual self – experiencing pain.

Being here and now, with life simply as it is, is the paradise we have been seeking.

HOW HAPPINESS HAPPENS

◆

We all say we want to be happy, but for many of us it's equally true to say that we want to be unhappy; we are addicted to our unhappiness. We are masters at making ourselves miserable, clinging to what makes us unhappy because we are afraid to let go of the familiar.

H APPINESS IS OUR NATURAL STATE. It happens when we stop making ourselves unhappy by believing in the stories the thinking mind throws up. Want to be happy? Then notice and let go of its opposite.

—————————————◆—————————————

If one is unhappy, one wants to know the reason why.

But it never occurs to one to ask why one is happy.

It is therefore unhappiness, rather than happiness,

that causes us to reflect upon our condition.

It is unhappiness that makes us think.

SANGHARAKSHITA (APHORISM)

—————————————◆—————————————

Happiness is the absence of unhappiness – it is not a thing in itself, and this is very important to understand. Happiness happens quite naturally when we cease our addiction to living in the future and past, which are full of promise and anxiety on the one hand, and regret and longing for on the other. When we cease getting distracted and agitated by our thinking minds, which recall the past and create the future, we come to live in the present moment, and in the present moment there are no problems and no anxiety. When we live in the present moment we are in touch with our deeper wisdom, and with wisdom we know how to live a good life.

AWARENESS PRACTICE

ON BEING PRESENT

Being in the present moment is the secret to a life of unconditional happiness and freedom. But how do we do it? How can we be present when our mind is all over the place? The key is simply to notice, without judgement or criticism, what takes you away from the present and then to return to the felt experience of the present.

Notice the tendency during the day to want to rush on to the next thing. For example, if you are cooking dinner, notice the urge to finish cooking and to be sitting eating it or watching TV later on. Notice what takes you away from the activity you are doing, and you will notice two things – thoughts and bodily sensations. Don't try to eliminate them or to change them – just notice them without judgement.

If we persevere in this simple practice, we learn how to let go of the thoughts and urges that push us around, leaving us free to choose our activities and how we do them.

How to Be Unhappy

We can make ourselves feel unhappy in so many ways. For example, what is our response if we're waiting for a bus and it's late? Are we fine with that or do we start complaining and getting into a bad mood? Or what if our friend says they will call and they don't. Are we OK with that and get on with what needs doing, maybe calling them and sorting it out? Or do we let the negative stories endlessly spin around in our heads, making ourselves unhappy as a consequence? It is our tendency to 'add on' to our experience that leads to our suffering. Most of the thinking around the event is unnecessary; it is this that is the problem.

It's the Little Things...

There are a million and one trivial things we can upset ourselves over during each and every day. But we need to look at these small things, so when the bigger things come along – such as our relationship breaking up, discovering we have a serious illness, or eventually of course our own death – we are better prepared to meet these circumstances.

By paying attention to the small, everyday upsets we can actually see that the upset comes from the stories in our own minds. When we are upset, we want life to be other than how it is. Watch how the mind keeps playing stories about how it wants things its own way, or how it convinces us that if things were different all would be well.

However, happiness doesn't happen through trying to change what is, but rather by accepting what is. If we come to see how we make ourselves unhappy, then happiness will be there ready and waiting for us. Rather than trying to change the 'bad' bits, relate to them in a kind and accepting way. We can stop trying to change ourselves and let ourselves be as we are; in this way we gradually and patiently bring the 'inner war' to an end.

The Key to Life

Stepping off the wheel of suffering is both the easiest and most difficult thing in the world. It's easy because all you do is notice the incessant thinking, and come back to whatever is happening right now. That may be simply listening to the traffic or some favourite music. It may be drinking your morning cup of tea or writing in the office. It doesn't matter what it is – what you are concerned with is breaking up the cycle of repetitive thinking.

It's difficult because we get so much perverse satisfaction from our stories. That is because we are the star of the show and it makes us feel very alive and important. To paraphrase Oscar Wilde, there is only one thing worse than incessantly thinking about oneself, and that's not incessantly thinking about oneself. The habitual tendency to experience ourselves through thought is great, and as a consequence we need patience, perseverance and kindness.

It is noticing in this way that leads to change. When we start to become aware of where most of our suffering comes from, it starts to fall away without us doing anything else about it. Our attachment to thought just dwindles away all by itself, leaving us happy and at ease.

Awareness is the key to life and it changes everything that needs changing.

AWARENESS PRACTICE

ON THOUGHTS

❋

Notice what stories the mind is telling you during the day. Observe where it wanders. There will be long periods when you forget to do this, but there is absolutely no need to give yourself a hard time, it is just what the mind does. If you find you are giving yourself a hard time, that again is the egoic mind telling its stories about how bad or useless you are, and you can notice that too.

Notice when you find yourself complaining and going over the same story again and again. Notice when you are talking yourself down – 'You stupid thing', or 'You are like this all the time.' Whatever your favourite stories are, notice them and step off the wheel that creates so much suffering.

A SIMPLE LIFE – A HAPPY LIFE

◆

It's so sad that we don't understand that each moment of
our lives – drinking coffee, walking down the street, reading the
paper – is it. Why don't we grasp this truth? We don't get it
because our little minds think that this second that we're living
has hundreds of seconds that preceded it, and hundreds of
seconds still to come. So we turn away from truly living our life.

FROM 'NOTHING SPECIAL: LIVING ZEN' BY CHARLOTTE JOKO BECK
HARPER SAN FRANCISCO, 1995

◆

*Simplicity is one of the most beautiful and joyful words in the
English language, and yet one that we are culturally cut off from
understanding and enjoying. The consumer society we live in has
made us feel that happiness lies in having things, and has failed to
teach us the happiness of not having things.*

ONE DISCUSSION that is often brought up by people who
come to my retreats and events is that of wanting to
live a simpler life. People complain about their lives being
stressful, hectic, over-complicated and with little or no room
for the simple things that they want to enjoy. They feel that
there is always the next thing to be done. As well as working,
running a home and perhaps looking after the children, there
is always a phone call to make, a bill to pay, always something
else that needs cleaning, perhaps another relative to visit.

I Have to Change!

When we find ourselves in this position we often look outside ourselves for what needs changing. Of course you need to do this, to look at your life to see what you can change. Can you work less? Can you cut down your spending so you don't have to work so hard? If you want to simplify your life, you need to assess it and to be honest about it.

However, only looking outside ourselves will not accomplish a great deal. This is because, until we face the sense of emptiness and incompleteness within, looking outside ourselves will mostly be in vain.

All of us to varying degrees have a feeling of incompleteness. Perhaps it's a feeling of not being fulfilled, maybe a sense that something needs to happen to us in order for us to feel happy and whole. As a consequence our lives become about trying to feel complete.

The Quest for Completeness

What do we do to feel complete? We overwork, we try to get people to like us, we try to find a lover who will fill the void, or we look for worthiness in status and reputation. We may end up as consumers buying bigger and more things, trying to numb out the feeling of incompleteness. We end up slaves to our desires, which in turn become habits. Instead of moving towards a sense of happiness and completeness, all these activities compound the sense of disharmony within. The more we only look outside ourselves for the solution, the greater the problem becomes. Before we know it we have set up a life where we are busy trying to avoid ourselves and end up more agitated and superficial as a result.

At some point it may dawn on us how busy and complicated our lives are, and we sense that we are running from ourselves. Usually at this point we realize just how exhausted all this busyness has made us. We yearn for some peace and simplicity in our lives.

Simple Desires

But how will we find simplicity? How do we start living simpler lives, and finding a sense of contentment and peace? To live a simple life we need to have simple desires. It's often not enough trying to renounce this, that and the other, if we are not learning how to embrace our desires and to stop being thrown around by them. It means looking at ourselves deeply and being honest about what is going on.

When we do this, we realize that the problem of feeling stressed and over-busy is because we are driven by thoughts and their accompanying emotions. If we are willing to be curious about what is going on we see that our minds are rarely at rest, our bodies rarely relaxed. We can notice for ourselves that, even before we have finished one thing, the mind is looking for the next – to keep us busy. We can observe how the body is constantly tense – and when the body is tense, the mind is likewise. It reads the body's tension, which to the mind means there is always something to look out for, always something dangerous to be aware of, it is on the alert. This in turn creates more tension in the body, and so on and on it goes. That is why our progress, to become truly relaxed and at ease, must involve both body and mind.

Sitting Still in a Quiet Room

It is so easy just to follow the mind and keep active, even if that activity is simply reading a newspaper, listening to music, calling a friend. Of course there is nothing wrong with these activities, they bring much pleasure, but we so often do it because we are incapable of doing nothing and just being. As Pascal said, 'The root of all man's problems is because he is unable to sit still in a quiet room by himself.'

Normally we are driven into activity by thoughts, impulses and urges. But if we take time to sit quietly, as in meditation, we find that we can actually watch them come and go. If we sit we can notice how thoughts and impulses arise and how we are moved to act. Normally we don't get to see this, we are simply thrown around by them like a leaf in the wind. We can get into such a frantic state, believing that we must do something or else our life will fall apart or something terrible will happen – awareness of this is crucial. We are so restless as a society because there is very little real awareness of our agitated minds, and the guilt and fear that are behind our activity.

A Wonderful Discovery

When we are willing to do this, time and again we realize for ourselves that much of our activity is carried out because we don't want to be with our feeling of incompleteness.

As this process continues, a change takes place. We find that because we are not jumping to every command the mind makes, it quietens down, and this is the beginning of the rest and ease we have actually been striving for. This is what it means to live a simple life. A simple mind leads to a simple life. That is where our attention needs to be. When we have a simple mind, a quiet mind, we are not pulled here and there into an endless stream of activity.

AWARENESS PRACTICE

ON BEING STILL

✻

For each of the next seven days, sit in a chair for ten minutes and notice the urges to get up. Be aware of the rationalizations that the mind comes up with to get you to do something. Notice what is actually happening when the impulse to get busy arises. The egoic mind hates being still because when there is stillness and observation it can be seen for what it is, and its reign as ruler is coming to an end.

CHAPTER TWO

STARTING
MEDITATION

One of the most effective ways of achieving the happiness and freedom you desire is to start a meditation practice. This isn't something complicated or special; you don't need particular skills or beliefs, simply the motivation to practise and the willingness to be open to whatever you discover. If you've never tried it before and feel a little unsure, just give it a go — you have nothing to lose and plenty to gain.

MEDITATION: NOT THIS, NOT THAT

◆

Through mindfulness meditation and awareness practices, you allow the unhappiness you have built around yourself to fall away, reconnecting you with your true and natural state of happiness. This chapter guides you through the process and explores what to expect from your meditation, and what not to expect.

As WE MEDITATE, we do feel better about ourselves, about life, which is great, but meditation is not about feeling a certain way. It's not about changing ourselves or about self-improvement. We do change and we certainly do learn and develop through meditation, which is wonderful, but that's not primarily what it's about. It's not about getting rid of our so-called bad qualities and replacing them with so-called good ones. It's not about having special or cosmic experiences. These may happen, but they are not what meditation is about. Meditation isn't about blanking our minds or ridding ourselves of thoughts. It's not about ridding ourselves of anything. Our minds do tend to be quieter as time goes on, which is a remarkable thing – but it's not what it's about.

A Certain Type...

Meditation is not about trying to change into a certain type of person. In fact, trying to change ourselves gets in the way, it's the self reinforcing the self. And it's certainly not about reaching some perceived ideal of perfection. This tendency to strive for perfection is one that 'spiritual' people can easily fall into. For example, when I became a Buddhist many years ago, I began to see myself as a spiritual person. I had the view that Buddhists had to be nice all the time – so I found myself smiling angelically at everybody I met. I was putting on a spiritual face and really it was a lie, because much of the time the last thing I felt like doing was smiling – at times I was pretty miserable. I also had the view that to be more spiritual I had to purify myself of what at the time I believed were my very un-spiritual bits. So, in my ignorance, I tried to banish what I thought were the unsavoury parts of my character. I would never admit to being angry – in fact, I just glossed over my anger with my angelic smiles. I didn't want to admit to having sexual thoughts and feelings because (I believed) these were the worldly desires that I had to purify myself of. Thankfully I saw the error of my ways...

Seeing Who We Are

Then what is meditation about? It's about *seeing*. This 'seeing' is done with our whole being (I also use the words 'watching' and 'noticing' to mean the same thing).

Meditation is about seeing who we are. It's about simply sitting (or any other meditative activity) and having a good honest look at who we think we are. It's about seeing that who we think we are is just a story.

It's about seeing what's going on right here and right now. It's about watching the experience that we are having and not getting lost in wishing for an experience that we're *not* having. Of course we tend to drift into fantasy, and that's fine, but we just notice that and return to our immediate felt experience of the body and its sensations.

A Simple Art

The art of meditation is simply to notice the bodily sensations and thoughts (the story that reinforces the 'I') that take us away from an open and direct experience of the moment.

Meditation is not about who we can become, but about who we are. It's not about changing ourselves into a different type of person, into a perfect person (there is no such thing as a perfect person), but about having a full-blooded experience of ourselves as we are, and accepting everything, absolutely everything about ourselves. This takes courage.

Meditation is an invitation. It's throwing open the doors and windows of being and allowing all aspects of ourselves to enter, without judging them in any way. It might be lust, joy, ill will, anxiety, resentment, bliss, violent thoughts, whatever, but they are all welcome.

Witness to the Truth

Everything passes in front of the impersonal witness. The witness doesn't judge, doesn't try to manipulate, but just sees the truth of whatever arises, which is impermanent and not who you really are. It is this ability to witness, irrespective of what is witnessed, that is the crux of meditation. It is this watching that leads to freedom. Out of watching (without trying to change or manipulate anything) our true nature unfolds.

Through watching, we come to see the story of who we think we are. As the story comes under the scrutiny of the impersonal witness, it begins to crumble. The story is really a story about *me*, about the 'I'. What we tend to do is to try to write a better story – that is, to become a better person. There is nothing wrong with this, of course, but it's not freedom, it's still in the realm of the story of *me*.

No-Self & Pure Awareness

No-self refers to the fact that there is not a fixed identity within, even though we may very much feel that there is. As we practise meditation, we learn that we are really a flow of ever-changing moods, feelings, emotions and thoughts and that 'behind' or 'beyond' thoughts and feelings there is awareness that remains unaffected by any amount of 'bad' experiences. We begin to realize that we are this *Pure Awareness* and as a consequence we relax in the face of thoughts and feelings. This is a very liberating experience.

The Essence of Meditation

True meditation is about seeing the truth of this, seeing that there is no 'doer of the deed' to be found; that there is nobody at central control running the show, and there never has been. This is the truth of no-self, the essence of meditation practice. Our experience is that 'I'm running the show', but when this is seen or even glimpsed to be just a story (thoughts) then we can relax and let life just happen – it does anyway. It is then seen that what we are is Pure Awareness itself, that we are whole and complete as we are, which is true happiness.

Life Lives Itself

Through meditation we do not get rid of the self that we believe exists inside our heads – rather, we see that it never existed in the first place. So long as there is a belief in the existence of a separate self inside us, we will strive anxiously to get life right. But when we start to see this misperception for what it is, we begin to understand ever more deeply that life lives itself. In other words, beyond our experience of our egoic mind there is a natural intelligence, a deeper wisdom, a compassionate presence, and as we realize this we let go and allow this natural intelligence to do what it will. This is what is really meant by being in the flow of life.

MEDITATION: HOW TO DO IT

Contrary to popular belief, meditation isn't about getting into some special state, or feeling something special. In fact it's not about feeling any particular way at all. It's not about feeling good (or bad), but about feeling just whatever we are feeling.

IF YOU THINK YOU NEED TO BE 'SPIRITUAL' in order to meditate, forget about it and simply start to bring awareness into your life. The same goes for knowing about Buddhism. If you are drawn to Buddhism, then pursue it by all means. But being a Buddhist is no guarantee that you will be practising well. The way to happiness is through awareness, and awareness is what you are and what you can bring to your life to enlighten it. So it doesn't matter whether you are an atheist, a Buddhist, a Christian. What matters is that you have an open mind and a curiosity to find out who you are. All you need is the motivation to practise meditation – and this you already have, or you wouldn't be reading this.

Meditation Posture

There are many misunderstandings surrounding meditation posture, but if we go back to basics and allow that to inform our practice, then all will be well. Meditation is about waking up, so any posture that allows us to wake up is best. Normally this means sitting upright, either on a chair or on a meditation

---

Perchance to Dream

You can meditate with your eyes open or closed – but remember that meditation is about waking up. Keeping your eyes open may help you to be more aware, while closing them may be a signal for sleeping and dreaming. Most people find that they are more likely to get lost in thoughts when they close their eyes. With eyes open it is a natural transition to the rest of our life. Try both ways to find out which is better.

---

cushion. Some people ask me if it's OK to meditate lying down. I ask if lying down helps them to be aware, and most admit that they tend to get sleepy when they lie down, so they have answered their own question. Of course, people who cannot sit upright comfortably because of physical problems may need to lie down; in this case there simply needs to be more vigilance about staying awake. Whatever your posture, all you need be is physically relaxed and mentally alert.

The Meditation

Find somewhere quiet and sit silently in your chosen position for ten minutes. Don't try to find the time, make the time. It's a good idea to sit at the same time each day if you can.

Once you are in position, simply pay attention to what-ever is happening in this moment. There is the breath, so pay attention to the breath. You may notice some sounds, maybe the refrigerator buzzing in the background, maybe some traffic, maybe an itchy nose. Then you may notice that you have been lost in daydreaming, fantasizing, planning, and all you do is come back to the feeling of your body and the breath. You just keep doing this over and over again. It's a good idea to set a timer for the duration of the sitting and stick to the time allotted, no more, no less.

Steady Progress

You may feel like sitting for fifteen minutes initially and after a few weeks working your way up to thirty minutes. Don't rush this process. Only increase your time when it feels right to do so. If you miss some sessions don't bully yourself, as this is completely contradictory to the attitude you are developing in sitting meditation. When you start to see the benefits of meditation, you will sit whether you feel like it or not.

Chanting

If you want to do a chanting meditation, then by all means chant. However, don't replace your silent meditation time with chanting or playing soothing music or anything else. If you want to do these things, do them in addition to your silent sitting practice.

Am I Doing This Right?

There is no right or wrong way in meditation. If you are paying attention, you are meditating. If you can notice the thought 'Am I doing this right?' and gently come back to the body and breath, then you are meditating. If you take a moment to notice when you have been unaware for a while and just acknowledge where the mind has been wandering to, then that is meditation. Remember, meditation is not about being aware of something special; it's not about developing some 'spiritual' state of mind, but about observing and experiencing yourself as you are, warts and all.

A Different 'You'

Over time you will notice a difference in the way you are in life. You may initially notice more clearly what triggers your anger and fear, for instance, and it is this awareness that eventually leads to the decreasing of these destructive emotions. But you must have a long-term view here. There may be times when it appears that you are getting angrier, for example, but this is not the case. What is happening is that all that is hidden is coming into awareness, and when it comes into awareness it begins to dissolve, like sugar in hot tea. So if you want to know whether you are doing it right, just look at your life and your relationships with other people.

SITTING IN THE MIDDLE

◆

Being present is really the heart of meditation. Our meditation is only as good as our ability to be present – but although it is necessary, presence isn't enough by itself. We need also to be curious. Presence and curiosity work together to create awareness.

IF WE ARE PRESENT, WE CAN BE CURIOUS; if we're curious, it helps keep us present. By curiosity I mean being interested in what's happening in the body and noticing our thoughts. The question really is – *are* we interested in what's going on?

Meditation, in my opinion, is so very simple – not easy – but so very simple. It comes down to being present with and witnessing our experience as it's happening. We don't need to get anywhere, or create a special state of mind, or feel a certain way, or *not* feel a certain way. We just sit with a sense of curiosity and witness whatever is arising. We may hear a bird singing, we notice that. We may hear a car pass by, we hear that too. Nothing complicated about it at all. We witness the breath, because it's there. We witness the sensations in the body, maybe a pressure in the side, maybe a tension in the belly, because it's there. There may be a twitch in the eye, we witness that; maybe our hands are cold, we witness that too. Why? Because this is our life as it is right now, this is reality. We may find that we are lost in thoughts, maybe anxious thoughts, so we bring awareness out of our spinning heads and into the felt experience of anxiety in the body. We can do the same with any other strong emotion too, experiencing the energy of it in the body. Not to eliminate it, but because it is there. Experiencing the energy of these states in the body tends gradually to lessen their power.

◆

When you make friends with the present moment,

you feel at home no matter where you are.

When you don't feel at home in the now, no matter

where you go, you will carry unease with you.

FROM 'STILLNESS SPEAKS: WHISPERS OF NOW' BY ECKHART TOLLE
HODDER MOBIUS, 2003

◆

Acceptance

We have no agenda for what should turn up in our meditation, so we don't make a choice for or against whatever does turn up. We don't judge anything as good or bad, we just notice. In this way we foster an attitude of acceptance of feelings, both pleasant and unpleasant. It is not to be confused with passivity – if we find ourselves getting lost in thoughts, fantasizing etc, we notice our thoughts and come back to our felt experience of the body and the breath.

This process allows us to experience our life as it's happening right now, rather than dreaming of a life we would rather have. Also, awareness of the body tends eventually to relax the body. There may well be times when long-held tensions 'rise to the surface' and make you feel more tense than usual, but these are good and necessary stages to go through.

Not Enemies After All

One thing you can do to help you to stay and watch your experience is to adopt an attitude of what I call *sitting in the middle*. When I go to sit, I have the intention to sit (or be) in the middle of my experience, no matter what my experience is. It may be fear, anxiety, joy, boredom, lust or ill will. But the point is to be right there with it, as it is, and not to get lost in wishing your experience, your life, to be different.

What slowly happens is that you become comfortable with the uncomfortable. You become intimate with yourself and no longer see feelings like anxiety, fear, lust as an enemy to be avoided. You come to realize that you don't need to treat them as enemies to rid yourself of, but as part of yourself that you can come to understand.

The Rewards of Curiosity

We can actually learn something about ourselves from these energies, if we are curious. Anxiety, for instance, might be telling us something about how we are living our lives. If we are fearful, for example, we can bring ourselves out of our spinning mind and into the feeling of fear in the body. Coming into the body actually allows this energy to dissipate.

Everything is meditation, there is nothing outside meditation, and we don't have to be in a certain state of mind before we can meditate. Whatever is in our awareness – that's it! That *is* meditation. Meditation is simply awareness.

The time will come

when, with elation

you will greet yourself arriving

at your own door, in your own mirror

and each will smile at the other's welcome,

and say, sit here. Eat.

You will love again the stranger who was your self.

Give wine. Give bread. Give back your heart

to itself, to the stranger who has loved you

all your life, whom you ignored

for another, who knows you by heart.

Take down the love letters from the bookshelf,

the photographs, the desperate notes,

peel your own image from the mirror.

Sit. Feast on your life.

DEREK WALCOTT

The Path to Freedom

As you become more intimate with your thoughts and your emotions, you begin to free yourself from their tyranny. You become more comfortable with them and within your body, too, and as you continue to watch you also begin to see their true nature, that they are not your self, that you are not merely your thoughts and emotions or even your body. You begin to see that you are something much vaster and more wonderful; you are Pure Awareness itself. This is true happiness and what meditation is essentially about.

The observation of experience is more important than what is observed. It is the art of watching experience – irrespective of what the experience is – that is going to lead us to freedom. If we cannot watch our experience and contain it and see it for what it really is, then we will be forever lost in our own turbulent subjective worlds.

It is good to realize that mindfulness is not a quick
fix; in fact it isn't a fix. We don't do it for a while
then stop. It's like eating; we don't just eat for a few weeks
then stop for life. We eat good food regularly; similarly we
practise mindfulness meditation regularly, and just
like good food it becomes part of our life diet.

SURYACITTA

Mind Chatter

You may feel that your mind is so busy that it will be a block to meditating – but if you have to wait until your mind is calm before you can meditate, what would be the point of meditation? If your mind is busy, then you can simply notice that your mind is busy. Thoughts are not a problem once we begin to leave them alone. When we can simply let them be without taking them all so seriously, they begin to die down of their own accord.

What Is Pure Awareness?

The human condition is one where we believe our thoughts and emotions to be who we are. We also believe our body to be who we are, or at least that it belongs to us. For example, when we are angry we say, 'I am angry', or if we are having lots of negative thoughts then we say, 'I am having negative thoughts.' We experience the body as part of our personal experience *here* as opposed to the world *out there*. But who is the 'I' who is having these thoughts, having these emotions, and relating to the body as though it owns it? The 'I' too is something that we are aware of. For instance, if we look at the wall there is awareness of it. If we look at the floor there is awareness of that too. Both the floor and wall have certain qualities such as shape, colour and density that can be observed and experienced. If we bring awareness closer to home we can also observe the body – this too has qualities that can be experienced. It has shape, colour and sensations. So it is with our feelings, thoughts and emotions – they can be observed and experienced too. If we come even closer, we can sense a 'me' or 'I' at the centre of all this, but we can also notice and pay attention to this 'I'.

Paying Attention to Awareness

So what is observing all of this, what is aware of all this, including the apparent 'I' at the centre? The answer is that it is awareness itself. If we pay attention to awareness we find no objective qualities to it, yet it definitely exists. What we find are the contents of awareness, and as a consequence we identify with some of them – the thoughts, the emotions and the body – as who we are. What we don't see is that we are the Pure Awareness within which they arise. It is pure because although it contains all things, it is never sullied by them. This is very difficult to grasp with the mind and really needs to be seen intuitively and contemplated.

OPENING TO OUR NATURAL GOODNESS

Meditation is basic and simple. We sit without a goal, without trying to achieve anything. We sit in the open space and allow everything in the body to be felt. Ultimately, the result of this is that we open ourselves to our natural goodness.

WE SIT HERE IN THE PRESENT and allow the breath to come in, and to go out, to come in, and to go out, then *bing!* – we find ourselves thinking about what we are going to do next birthday. Then we label that thought as just 'thinking'. Then we find awareness is back with the body and breath. We find it back with life as it is, tasting, feeling, hearing, seeing and allowing reality to be just what it is.

Through this simple activity our dignity arises – not a false, manufactured dignity, but our true dignity. This happens because we are being honest and genuine with ourselves, without contrivance. We are not trying to appear dignified, friendly, kind, calm or anything, we just *are*.

Welcome to One & All

When you sit in this way you don't choose your experience, you are not saying, 'Oh, I want this pleasant experience and not that nasty, agitated one.' All experiences are welcome. This attitude opens you to your natural goodness and allows kindness to arise towards your suffering and yourself.

You accept whatever comes into your space – why reject it? You accept that the sky is blue, that water is wet, that tea is pleasant or unpleasant, so you can accept yourself too.

Our Ever-Present Goodness

So often we fight with ourselves, we turn away from our present experience of reality to hopeless dreaming and scheming about how we would like to be, or how we think we should be. How often have you turned away from your own heart, because you were scared of what you might find? When we turn away like this, we turn away from our natural goodness.

Our natural goodness is always here. It is already present behind all the distractions and deceptions that we engage in. All these manipulations are pointless strategies to avoid how life is, and the joy it reveals.

Time to Face Up

How often have you looked in the mirror and stayed looking even when the self-consciousness arises? How often do you distract yourself by reading newspapers, watching TV, using the phone or just being a bit dozy?

If we are willing to face our present experience, we find that slowly we are opening to our natural goodness. We open to the innate self-love that awaits us. I remember for many years I was told that I needed to love myself more than I did. And I knew this was true, but nobody was able to tell me how to do it – they were able to tell me what was needed, but not how to do it. What I realized at some point is that self-love is already there, it arises when we stop playing the game of deception and distraction and allow ourselves to simply be with how life is.

Overcoming Fear

If we are honest we will know that we are constantly afraid of ourselves, we will see that we find it difficult to be naturally upright. We are so ashamed. Some of us are ashamed of our jobs, some ashamed of our education, ashamed of our class, ashamed of our feelings, ashamed of who we are. And we tend to make the problem worse by running away from these feelings of shame. As we meditate, we allow all those uncomfortable feelings to arise – we allow them their rightful place.

This is the way to become at ease and to rest in your natural goodness, your natural loving heart. Your natural loving heart doesn't reject shame, doesn't reject your aggression or fear...that wouldn't be very loving, would it! Your loving heart accepts them fully and soothes them.

Let It Be...

The spirit of meditation is about letting yourself be. If you have nice thoughts, let them be. If you have nasty thoughts, let them be. You don't have to get rid of thoughts, but simply leave them alone. In Tolstoy's *Anna Karenina*, there is a saying,

'I know not myself but my appetites.' This is true for most of us. We tend to know ourselves through our thoughts, feelings, desires and beliefs, not realizing there is a deeper beauty behind all these uncertain phenomena. But if we are willing to do what's necessary and trust that there is something behind these states of mind, then we will begin to taste what it is like to be truly human. We will naturally find our way home, to the restful place that we never left.

Letting thoughts and feelings be, in the way described, is what is meant by renunciation – letting go of the petty worries and preoccupations that so often overtake us.

IN THIS SPACE

We can see meditation as a big space, a big container in which we are sitting. What do we find in this space? We find thoughts and feelings, sounds and sensations. And after a time we begin to find what we are seeking. We find awareness, wisdom – and happiness.

IN OUR SPACE WE HEAR SOUNDS, maybe the sound of the heating system in the background, for example. Maybe we can hear the wind outside, or the sound of cars in the distance. If we have our eyes open, we see in this space the floor with its particular pattern, and people sitting around us. In this space there may be the smell of incense and the sensation of saliva in our mouths.

Being with Reality

In this space there are thoughts coming and going; maybe we get lost in some and others we see pass by. There are also bodily sensations – maybe a tension, perhaps an itch. In this space there might be a feeling of calm and contentment or maybe there's a sense of agitation and worry. Can we simply sit and be with reality, which is what we have just decided to do, and not get caught up with thoughts of enlightenment and all that it is supposed to bring? Instead of striving for enlightenment, can we just experience the sound of the heating, the feeling of sadness or the sensation of resistance to being here?

Can we let all this happen without interfering or trying to make ourselves feel better or more comfortable? Our experience is that all this is happening to *me*, a little person inside this head or body. But is this really the case? If we are prepared to really look we will see that the wonder of life is happening, but there is not a person or a *me* inside that it is happening to. It is Pure Awareness that is hearing, smelling or feeling everything, including the '*me*'.

Life Is a Big Space

This is the great deception. It is from this mistaken belief in the *me* that all our troubles arise. This sense of *me* or self always feels a lack, so we run through life trying to fill this lack with anything and everything, always to no avail. If we are willing to sit and pay attention, if we are willing to really listen to each moment, we can see that there is just hearing without anybody hearing, feeling without anybody feeling, living without anybody living.

We can see life in the same way as we see meditation. We can see our life as a big space where anything and everything can enter. Sometimes what enters is joy, sometimes sadness and fear. Sometimes there is work to be done and sometimes there's the need for rest. Sometimes what enters are people whom we dislike and other times people we love. Can we notice the countless mental and bodily reactions that we have during our days? If we can watch all our reactions to whatever enters this space without believing our judgements and opinions, then a greater wisdom slowly enters our life. It is a wisdom we can trust in. This wisdom is not a thing – it contains all things.

◆

It's not that 'I' hear the birds, it's just hearing the birds.
Let yourself be hearing, seeing, thinking. It is the false 'I'
that interrupts the wonder with the constant desire to think
about 'I'. And all the while THE WONDER is occurring:
the birds sing, the cars go by, the body sensations continue,
the heart is beating – life is a second-by-second miracle.
But dreaming our 'I' dreams we miss it.

FROM 'EVERYDAY ZEN' BY CHARLOTTE JOKO BECK
THORSONS, 1997

◆

Meditation & Happiness

By now, you may be wondering quite how meditation leads to happiness, when it seems to be less about trying to feel good and more about discovering and accepting who we are. The answer is that we are unhappy because we are unaware, so anything that brings about a profound shift in awareness is of paramount importance with regard to happiness. The best single activity that I know of for bringing about this shift in awareness is meditation.

But it's not wrong to seek happiness through meditation. The desire to be happy is what draws us towards meditation. However, what happens is a slow process of maturation. As we have seen, our desire for happiness often takes us into the realm of acquiring objects, status, a lifestyle, a partner. These things can be immensely joyful and meaningful, however at some point we see that they do not bring us the lasting happiness that we desire. If we meditate honestly, we come to see that complete happiness or absolute fulfilment can never be achieved by the 'trappings' of the outer world. When we reach this point it is the golden opportunity of a lifetime. We may slowly give up striving after the million and one things and begin to explore more deeply our own minds and hearts. In other words, we let go of the effort to make happiness happen through acquisition and see

The desire to be happy is what draws us towards meditation.

that happiness happens when we stop trying to make it happen. When this realization takes place, and we open to unconditional happiness, we sit and wonder that this absolute treasure is what we have been seeking all the time.

The Beginning of Peace

During meditation, we don't run away from anything and we don't run after anything, we allow everything to be simply as it is. We may notice our desire to change something that we don't like and we allow that to be also. This is a practice of acceptance, of surrender. We simply give up the egoic will to do anything, to cultivate anything, to change anything. As we practise in this way we realize that we are more able to experience feelings and emotions without being disturbed by them. This is the beginning of peace.

We are unhappy because
we are unaware...

CHAPTER THREE

ACCEPTING, NOT CHANGING

*How many times a day do we think or feel
'I don't want to be here', 'I don't want to feel like this',
'I don't want this to be happening to me'? If we're
in this state then we are resisting life, creating more
pain for ourselves by wishing things to be different.
It's far better to change what we can and accept fully
what we can't. If we can accept life, accept ourselves,
this is the end of conflict. Happiness and freedom
are present right now if only we can learn to
accept the 'unacceptable'.*

DON'T CHANGE

There is a certain relief in change, even though
it be from bad to worse! As I have often found in
travelling in a stagecoach, that it is often a comfort
to shift one's position, and be bruised in a new place.

FROM 'TALES OF A TRAVELLER' BY WASHINGTON IRVING
(UNDER THE PSEUDONYM OF GEOFFREY CRAYON)
JOHN MURRAY, 1824

It's common to see meditation and spiritual practice as a way of changing ourselves, and this is understandable. If we feel unworthy about ourselves, we will want to feel worthy. If we're unhappy, we'll want to be happy, and if we feel stuck, we'll want to be free.

I T'S EASY TO FALL INTO THE TRAP of believing that if we're to attain happiness then we need to change into a different, better, person. This is not helpful.

When we adopt this attitude we can so easily get caught up in the future... 'I'll be happy when I've changed all these things about myself.' But we can be content now, be happy now, with how life is now; in fact we can *only* be happy now.

A Battle You Can't Win

Some years ago, I had a client who was anxious to change (see panel above right), but was approaching it all wrong.

> **I Tried...**
>
> I was a neurotic for years. I was nervous, anxious and scared. Everyone kept telling me to change, to love myself. As a result I felt self-conscious, resentful and trapped. I wanted to change. I tried and tried, but I couldn't.

I encouraged him to stop trying to change and to let himself be what he is. Soon he saw that battling with himself wasn't working and he relaxed. That was all the change he needed.

It seems to me that people can easily get into trying to change through pushing and battling with themselves. Often I notice that the constant urge to change simply exhausts us and leaves us feeling despondent. It doesn't have to be like that. We can rest in who we are right now with all our neurotic little ways – they're OK, we're OK, we don't need fixing. This is not a licence for hurtful behaviour. Accepting oneself doesn't mean expressing oneself when inappropriate. It actually works to the contrary; if we accept and experience things like anger and fear, then we are far less likely to express it or feel overwhelmed by it.

Under the Spotlight
What do we do? It is so simple, though I find a lot of people just don't believe it can be...we simply watch ourselves.

We watch all our little ways, all our self-centred thinking and actions, and let the light of awareness change us. We don't change ourselves, but change happens effortlessly by watching ourselves; change happens through awareness and understanding. This is not intellectual analysis. We just watch ourselves without judgement.

If we do judge ourselves, that is watched too. Everything comes under the spotlight of awareness.

Winning the Tug of War

For example, if I'm in a queue and feeling impatient to reach the counter, the natural thing to do is to *try* to be patient, to impose patience on impatience. This, however, can end up in a sort of tug of war – impatience-patience, impatience-patience – over and over again. But instead of trying to change the impatience or fight with it, what I can do is become intimate with it. This means feeling it and watching the thoughts around it. The lovely thing that can be discovered here is that patience is waiting 'just behind' the impatience – waiting to shine forth. I don't need to impose it.

This happens with other aspects of ourselves too. If we're nervous around a certain person it's very easy to try to fight it, or try to change it, or to pretend it's not there. Instead of doing this, turn towards it and become intimate with it. Doing this eases the inner conflict and allows us to see its impermanent nature and that it is not who we really are.

An Unexpected Transformation

We don't need to concern ourselves with how we are going to become, with what we are going to change into. We can leave that to our natural intelligence, our innate wisdom, which is the awareness itself that is doing the watching.

When we let go in this way and stop trying to change ourselves, we discover something wonderful. We discover that not trying to change ourselves actually brings about a great transformation. We start to see our 'difficult areas' not as enemies to be repressed, feared or eliminated (which actually empowers them), but as aspects of ourselves that simply need awareness, that need understanding. This act of experiencing and watching instead of interfering brings us to peace; brings the struggle to an end. We can let awareness bring us to rest, we can let awareness bring us to reality, then we won't be there, and this is freedom.

The Ego's Investment

I'm often asked, 'But if I don't try to change myself isn't there a danger that I end up doing nothing, maybe being a couch potato, maybe even ending up homeless?'

It's not a danger, but a fear. The attitude of trying to change is really a way of keeping up the illusion that we are in control of life. Trying to change into a future ideal is the ego investing in the future. The ego creates time and loves to invest in it, and in this way it secures its survival.

Little Me

The *little me* is the voice in our head that commentates on life all day long. Identifying with this little voice is what causes us much distress. It tries to convince us that it has all the answers to our problems when in fact it is part of the problem itself. It is born from the need to be somebody as we are growing up. I also use the terms *ego*, *egoic mind* and the *self*. This is because different terms resonate with different people – but they refer to the same thing.

Trying may result in change, but it's still in the realm of the ego, in the realm of the self, of *little me*. What we can end up doing is just rewriting the story of *me*; a so-called better and nobler story, but it's still about *me*, it's not freedom. What is needed is to watch the ego, what is needed is to watch the *me*, without judgement and criticism, and let it dissolve in the light of awareness. As the ego (the story of me) is watched, what we find is more and more openness, more and more sensitivity to life, more and more freedom.

Give Up the Struggle

What we can do is let go and relax. It's like being on a roller-coaster ride and holding on for dear life to the steering wheel up front. As the car turns we turn the wheel, thinking we are in control of it. But the wheel is only a pretend one and the car is turning where it likes anyway. If we let go we can sit back, relax and enjoy the ride. Give our life over to awareness; give up the struggle and be happy.

Stop Beating Yourself Up!

Self-criticism is a very common tendency. The usual way of approaching this is to give ourselves a hard time for giving ourselves a hard time. We perversely believe that digging further down into the hole will get us out of the hole. We like to pile on the agony.

Instead, simply notice the voice and the tone of the voice in your head. When you are talking to yourself in that condemnatory way, acknowledge that. Just say to yourself, 'I'm talking harshly to myself.' Another approach is to smile at the critical voice. Don't get into a war with it. You don't end a war by going to war. If there's a fire and you want it to go out, you need to let it burn itself out of fuel. Getting mad at yourself is throwing fuel on the fire. Ask yourself how it feels when you're being critical of yourself. Once you really start to see that the purpose it serves is to make you feel depressed, then slowly it will fall away. But until then a part of you thinks that it's a necessary thing and is there to protect you.

Don't fight it. Sit down a few times a week and say hello to the critical part of yourself. Ask it how it feels. Listen to its concerns. Let it reveal itself to you.

Changing Our Actions

When I say that the aim of meditation is not to change ourselves, I am primarily referring to our inner world. I encourage people to accept themselves unconditionally. However, in the world of our actions it is slightly different. For example, if we find ourselves stealing, we'd best stop otherwise we end up in prison, simple as that. With things like smoking and drinking, there may come a time when the desire to stop is strong enough and it happens. However, if we use so-called willpower, the craving often just finds an outlet somewhere else – for example, a lot of ex-smokers overeat instead and gain weight. The way I suggest is that of awareness. For example, when we want to smoke there is a craving to do so. There is also the craving not to smoke, so immediately we have a conflict. A part of 'me' wants to smoke and a part of 'me' doesn't want to smoke. Try to observe the whole process without judgement or opinion – when you have the urge to smoke, feel and observe that urge; when you have the urge to stop, feel and observe that too.

Observing Desire

This is open, relaxed seeing, without any agenda. Quite often when we crave something our attention goes to the object of craving. We have an incorrect belief that the object will satisfy the desire. But if we're honest we will admit that while we may get a temporary feeling of fulfilment, it rarely lasts long.

What I am suggesting is that we take our attention to the desire itself. If I'm craving a cigarette, for example, instead of just reaching for the box I can spend a minute or two feeling the desire to have one. I can notice where I feel it. I can observe the rationalizations that go through the mind. I can feel the different qualities of the desire. Maybe I notice the contradictory voices on the one hand urging me to have one, and on the other to resist. If I can allow the whole show to reveal itself to awareness, what I find are bodily sensations and thoughts – nothing more, nothing less. If we believe them, we give them power over us. Over time, the awareness grows and we find our addictions slowly becoming easier to deal with, not through effort, but through insight.

It is the same with anger and other strong emotions. If we can acknowledge that we are angry and feel the anger in the body, we are less likely to repress it or express it.

*I encourage people to
accept themselves unconditionally.*

THE FEELING BODY

◆

The sensations we experience in our bodies become so familiar that often we believe they are part of who we are and pay no attention to them. But our personal histories are stored within our bodies as positive or negative energies, so we need to give awareness to these sensations and allow them to reveal their messages.

THE CONCRETE BLOCK IN THE STORY (see panel below) represents our own body, our own being. The looking around represents our restless looking outside ourselves for

---

The Prison Cell

Imagine you are in a prison cell, and along one wall is a long concrete block. This is where you are to rest and sleep, but it looks very uncomfortable. So you put off the moment of taking to your bed. You look around for somewhere more comfortable to lie, but you know that there isn't anywhere else. You get very tired and finally you lie on the block. It's hard and cold, but there is nowhere else to rest. After a while you realize it's not as bad as you thought. In fact, it is quite comfortable and at last you stop looking for somewhere else and settle with what you have. After a while you realize that it wasn't a concrete block after all, but a comfortable mattress.

---

someone or something to take care of us so that we don't have to feel any pain. But if we are willing to rest on what appears to be a concrete block (our own bodily experience), then we realize that it is the only place where we will ever find peace and happiness. We come to see that if we can't find peace in our own body with all its feelings and emotions, where can we find it? This is a great realization. It is a realization that the only way to happiness and freedom is right here, right now, in our own being with all its many uncomfortable qualities.

Practising Body Awareness

Being uncomfortable with our own feelings and emotions is the thing that I notice the most. Whether we are new to spiritual practice or very experienced, our work means moving from being ill at ease in our body to being comfortable in it. This is essential if we are to live a happy and satisfying life. Becoming comfortable with all our bodily sensations can be done very effectively through body awareness.

We need to remember that awareness practice is not about reaching a certain stage or experiencing a certain state of mind, but about having a full-blooded, authentic experience of ourselves as we are and being able to observe ourselves. All we need to do is to feel our body with awareness, to experience whatever sensations are alive in the body now, including the breath. Body awareness also includes other senses, such as hearing, so we can bring mindfulness to simply listening.

A Healing Effect

One of the many benefits of body awareness is that it allows integration and healing to happen. We will all have certain aspects of ourselves that we find unacceptable, which means we are uncomfortable with them. Perhaps we have painful memories; we may have long-held hurt from the past, or resentments going back in some cases for decades. What we may want to do is trace back and know why we are the person we are. I think many therapies encourage this. In some cases, of course, it may be appropriate if done with skill and care. This is not analysis; it is the end of analysis. In awareness practice we are not trying to work out all the reasons why we are the person we are.

Releasing the Past

What we need to remember is that all this hurt and all these memories are present right here in the body. Every thought we have and every incident in our life has an effect on the body. If it's a kind thought or event, the body responds positively by relaxing or opening up. If it's a nasty thought or painful event, then the opposite happens, it contracts. Most of us will have experienced that, as we bring awareness into the tensions and contractions of the body, it eventually relaxes and releases the energy stored. We may start jerking as a consequence of this, or memories may arise, tears may flow, but what is happening is that the unresolved issues of the past, the tensions that we may have carried around for years, are slowly being resolved and dissolved. This happens because we are no longer ignoring the body, but giving it the attention it deserves. We could even say that we are listening to the body and the reward of that listening is the healing of (quite often unacknowledged) pain that we have carried around for years. Also, as the tensions and contractions begin to release we will experience more energy – more vitality and aliveness. It can be a 'welcome to life' experience.

Expecting an epiphany – some single moment of insight that will forever banish the experience of fear, anger, neediness – may prevent us from noticing the slow and almost imperceptible ways spiritual practice subtly transforms us. With patience and perseverance our habitual reactive patterns slowly erode, until one day we find ourselves in a situation that had always made us anxious – and we notice the anxiety is simply gone.

FROM 'SAYING YES TO LIFE (EVEN THE HARD PARTS)' BY EZRA BAYDA
WISDOM PUBLICATIONS, 2005

Here's How It's Done…

It's easy to speak of body awareness, but how exactly do we do it? What I mean by the term is the act of listening to the body and bringing a quality of warm creative interest to the feelings you encounter. This is not thinking about the body, nor is it relating to an image we have of it in our minds. What body awareness means is to feel the body with the body. This is not a technique that can be taught, but rather the outcome if we maintain a spirit of curiosity about ourselves.

For instance, we may be experiencing a sensation of something vaguely uncomfortable in our belly. All we need do in this situation is to allow the feeling to be there; we need first to accept the feeling of discomfort. Allow it to be there like you allow the breath to be there. What the sensation wants is to release itself – so we allow it to be there, we allow it to arise into consciousness and to pass away. Our job is not to interfere with it, but to be a space for it.

This is not something that is done only on our meditation cushion; it can be done while buying our biscuits at the local grocer's, or talking to a friend.

Living Life, Not Missing It

The emotional healing that comes from body awareness is a wonderful thing; however, the greatest benefit is that it allows us to be present with life while it's happening. Much of the time we live a life of abstraction – that is, we live our lives in our heads. We prefer to think about life than to feel it or live it. We often get lost in thinking about how we would like our life to be, or how it could be or, even worse, how it should be. What's happening while we're doing this? Life is going on and we are missing it. This doesn't mean that we don't think about our life when appropriate, but that we don't get lost in constant fantasy about it.

If we allow ourselves to be constantly lost in our thinking minds, we will be forever in conflict, always ill at ease.

Did I Lock the Car?

I remember many years ago sitting in a cinema with my new girlfriend. The place was full and everyone seemed rapt in the movie. Suddenly I had a moment of panic. I had just got my new car, which I was so very proud of and attached to. The panic was created by a thought, 'Did I lock my car?' 'Of course I locked the car,' I assured myself, 'just enjoy the film.'

I relaxed for a few moments, but then the thought came back, 'Are you sure, you know what this area is like for thefts.' 'For goodness sake, shut up,' replied the panic voice. On and on this dialogue continued in my mind. I was sitting there watching this great movie while this other movie played out inside my head, and I remember getting very agitated.

I couldn't leave the cinema and couldn't enjoy what was going to be a night of great entertainment – all because I was caught up in my thoughts. I had two choices, either to do something about it and go out and check (in this case, however, I didn't want to appear uncool), or to forget it and to sit and enjoy the movie. I couldn't do either, so I sat in conflict for much of the show, and later felt very uncool indeed.

Lost in Thought

Worry and being caught up in anxious thoughts is a state of inertia. It's a state of being stuck in our neurotic thinking, which leads to a feeling of helplessness.

It's not thinking that's the problem, but the identification with thinking. It's when we believe all our thoughts that the trouble starts. Through awareness, we are more capable of discerning the difference between thoughts imbued with wisdom and those that are part of destructive patterns. When we cease believing all our thoughts the mind becomes quiet, and a quiet mind is an intuitive mind.

Making the Transition to Feeling

When you first practise body awareness, you may find that your body responds by feeling numb. As we grow up, we all experience hurt and find the world a threatening place to varying degrees. As a consequence we close down our feelings to avoid experiencing them. This is done through bodily contracting, and over time this becomes the body's default position. We may become unable to feel and end up living an abstract life in our heads. What we need to do is to experience the defensive bodily contraction as it is. That's why bodily awareness – that is, experiencing the body and all its tensions in meditation – is absolutely essential. Over time this holding, this bodily contraction dissolves and our feelings start to be experienced again. However, this cannot be rushed.

Feeling Is Living

The view we may have taken on when young is that feeling equals being hurt. What we need to realize is that feeling means being alive. When the bodily contraction begins to dissolve, there is quite naturally an experience of ease and relaxation in one's being. We feel more at ease with ourselves, and the separation between self and others begins to soften. It's like putting ice cubes out in the sun – they dissolve in their own time without any interference from us.

One of the things I have noticed with many people is that we try to resolve our suffering only on the mental level. But the suffering exists on both the mental and the physical levels, and if we miss out on the physical healing there is no chance of true healing and happiness.

AWARENESS PRACTICE

ON EMOTIONS

❋

Next time you experience a strong emotion like fear or anger, turn towards it and feel its different qualities in the body. Be curious instead of running away from it. Approach it with gentleness and courage, without judging it as good or bad.

Our troublesome emotions have messages. That's why they are troublesome. If we learn to be with our emotions and feelings with curiosity, we can let them reveal their messages to us, thereby releasing them.

RADICAL SELF-ACCEPTANCE

◆

We all have aspects of ourselves that we are uncomfortable with. We may experience anger, fear, jealousy, sadness; we may have nasty thoughts about others or about ourselves. We can even make the painful experiences worse by feeling bad about having them at all.

I N THIS SCENARIO we are creating more and more unnecessary suffering for ourselves. But it doesn't have to be like this. We don't need to feel bad about feeling anything. All these aspects of ourselves are fine, they're not bad.

If we think our thoughts and feelings are bad or that we're a bad person for having them, we can so easily repress them. Repression can lead to illness and a loss of vitality. It prevents us from living a full and happy life.

Say 'Yes'

We can come to accept all these aspects of ourselves; we can say 'yes' to everything. There is absolutely nothing about us that is not worthy of acceptance.

So say 'yes' to the anger, 'yes' to sadness, 'yes' to resentment, 'yes' to the nasty thoughts about somebody, 'yes' to the joy we feel with a friend. Say 'yes' to your present experience, no matter what it is. This does not necessarily mean expressing your feeling, but it means experiencing it. If you can experience it you are less likely to express it.

How Does It Feel?

When we have a painful experience it's very easy to fight it, or resist it, or to pretend it's not there. We will do anything but face up to our present felt experience. But if we want to be free and happy we need to do just this. Instead of running from experience, we can become intimate with it by turning towards it and feeling it. What does the fear feel like? What does anger feel like? What does joy feel like? Where do we feel sadness? Whatever it is, we can become intimate with it. We can learn to stay with the felt experience and allow it to show its face to us.

We Are the Awareness

When we watch and experience in this way, we begin to see something quite remarkable – that we are not the anger, we are not the fear. If the fear can be watched objectively, then it cannot be who we are. If the anger can be watched, then that too is not who we are. Normally we may assume that 'I'm angry' or 'I'm afraid', but that isn't how it is. The anger isn't who we are; however, we do need to experience the emotion and not repress it. This experiencing and watching help us to wake up from identification with the various states of mind that are experienced. We then begin to discover something quite wonderful, that we are the awareness that is doing the watching. We see that we are something much more vast and wonderful than our usual small and constricted self.

Acceptance

What we are doing here is learning to experience and to open up to who we are. We are learning to accept our life as it is, to accept our experience as it is, not to change it, not to rid ourselves of our experience, but to understand it. This brings about a great transformation, and we no longer see fear, anger etc as the hidden enemy to be avoided. It's similar to being intimate with a person. Once we become familiar with them, once we become intimate with them, we are much more comfortable around them.

How to Accept

Acceptance is simple – there is nothing difficult or compli-cated about it at all. What is difficult is living a life of resistance, which is the opposite of acceptance. To accept, we simply bring awareness to where we are resisting. If we are resisting anything at all, a feeling of tension or constriction in the body will reflect it. We don't need to try to relax the tension, but to accept and feel it. Allow it to be there exactly as it is. There is no need to change it or try to eliminate it. In fact, if we can let it be, it may even open up and reveal its little treasure. It's telling us something about ourselves.

There is much more to acceptance than merely accepting our present experience. What we need to do is to accept that we are more than the self-centred little being that may be our usual experience. We can accept that we are Pure

---

Learn to Play

It's important to take time out and do the simple things that we love to do – the things that satisfy our hearts. In other words, we need to learn to play. As we meditate, we will find things out about ourselves and discover what it is that we do and don't enjoy.

Awareness itself. We can accept that we are the space or consciousness in which everything appears. We can accept that we are everything and at the same time we are nothing. This is freedom.

AWARENESS PRACTICE

ON ACCEPTANCE

✻

Whenever you are feeling upset, bring awareness into the body and attend to the upset. Ask yourself, 'What's happening right now?' or 'What does this feel like?' Simply stay with the feeling of upset in your body. Don't try to change it or to get rid of it, but gently feel it and let it be. Observe where it is you feel it. Observe its different qualities. Observe how it changes and moves around the body ever so slightly.

This is the way of acceptance and helps bring the 'inner war' to an end, bringing peace and rest into your life.

TRUSTING IN AWARENESS

◆

We are all addicted to thinking about life. It takes a lot of trust to stop trying to work everything out and simply to dwell in the present moment; but behind the usual incessant thinking that goes on in our heads is a greater intelligence in which we can trust.

IN LIFE WE MAY TRUST IN OUR ABILITY to become what we want to become. For instance, we may want to become a doctor, so we train and hopefully we qualify. Or we may want to paint, so we learn to paint, and so on. In life we have an agenda and we try to follow it through to the best of our ability, and this is absolutely fine.

When we enter into spiritual practice we tend to do a similar thing. We bring an agenda to our practice as to how we want to be in the future, but if we practise well this agenda is doomed to failure. It's OK to have an agenda for a while as it can motivate us to start to practise, but it will never be fulfilled, because agendas are of the ego: the *little me*. The ego always wants to become somebody, but practice is not about becoming somebody. Practice is about getting to know your-self and becoming free from suffering by doing so. As we have seen, this freedom can't be achieved through our usual type of striving. Our true, happy, nature can be discovered only when we give up the struggle to be better, to be someone different. We understand this intellectually – but there is a problem...

Going Beyond the Intellect

Most of us in the West have complicated and clever minds, and so we tend to complicate spiritual practice. Most of us trust not in the simple act of being aware, but in the power of the analytical mind. We believe that if we can understand something well enough intellectually, then that is what spiritual practice is about.

It's a good thing to understand something intellectually, but we must move beyond the intellect and trust in something else, and that something else is wisdom, intuitive awareness, our deepest knowing, God – it can have any name, call it what you will. It's trusting in that indefinable knowing that lies deep in our being. This is what the Buddha and other great teachers were telling us. They wanted us to be a light unto ourselves and not to depend upon hearsay or to rely upon tradition. They wanted us to trust in our own wisdom.

Trust in Awareness

We can give up the idea of trying to change ourselves. We can let go of trying to rid ourselves of aspects that we don't like, and of trying to add anything on to ourselves. This is just aversion and attachment in more subtle forms. This doesn't mean that we don't change through spiritual practice; we change radically. But we can let change happen naturally as a result of our practice of awareness. For instance, if we have a tendency to unkindness (of course we do our best not to be unkind), instead of getting into a war with it – 'I shouldn't be like this, I need to get rid of this' – we can trust in the awareness of it. If we can let it be, it arises and passes away and eventually runs out of fuel if we allow it to. It's crucial here, of course, not to get caught up in the unkind thoughts. If we do, we tend to express and cause pain to others and ourselves.

Trying to change is another way of saying, 'I'm not good enough, and I need to change myself in order to be good enough.' We can give up the idea that we need to change, and rest in who we are right now.

Trust in Simply Knowing

We can simply *know* whatever is happening right now. This knowing includes everything and excludes nothing. If we have a nasty thought, we can know that; if we have a nice thought, we can know that too. Practice isn't about being in a particular state, but simply knowing the state we are in. This is so simple and direct and takes no thinking about.

Many people don't believe that practice is this simple. 'But surely I need to think about my practice, I need to read loads of books, I need to purify myself of all my bad karma.' All these thoughts and questions can be witnessed and left alone. If thoughts arise about our life that seem important to act on, then of course we do that. Otherwise, we can simply know that a thought is or has been present. Simply know, experience and trust in that direct knowing of each moment.

AWARENESS PRACTICE

ON TRUST

❋

Sit in your meditation posture each day and simply trust in the act of non-doing. While sitting, notice the urge to do something, to make something happen. Notice the urge to fix things, or to change an uncomfortable feeling. Notice all the subtle strategies to avoid being with your experience as it is.

When we start to see the way the mind is endlessly pulling us away from the present moment, we weaken its power. Over time we notice that we are more present and so begin to experience more ease and peace in our life.

The Parable of the Two Arrows

We can use what we learn in meditation to help us through the inevitable tough times in life. The parable of the two arrows illustrates this. The first arrow – the one that stabs us in the heart – represents the things over which we have little or no control, from minor things like missing a train to the major things like losing our job. And what do we usually do? We pick up a second arrow and stab ourselves over and again with our judgements, opinions and stories. We may wallow in thoughts like, 'I'll never get another job – it's useless.' From now on, *notice* when you reach for the second arrow.

CHAPTER FOUR

MEETING YOUR EMOTIONS

Our lives are full of emotions, feelings and simply 'ways of being'. Our instinct is to welcome the 'positive' ones, such as love and joy and all they embrace, and to fear the 'negative' ones — of which the greatest is perhaps fear itself. But fear, loneliness, worry, desire and blaming can all be overcome by bringing awareness to them, experiencing them, knowing them.

This being human is a guest house.
Every morning a new arrival.

A joy, a depression, a meanness,
some momentary awareness comes
As an unexpected visitor.

Welcome and entertain them all!
Even if they're a crowd of sorrows,
who violently sweep your house
empty of its furniture,
still treat each guest honorably.
He may be clearing you out
for some new delight.

The dark thought, the shame, the malice,
meet them at the door laughing,
and invite them in.

Be grateful for whoever comes,
because each has been sent
as a guide from beyond.

RUMI (TRANSLATED BY COLEMAN BARKS)

FEAR – IT'S NOT WHAT YOU THINK IT IS

Fear is present in all of our lives. It's an emotion that keeps us small, it prevents us from living open, happy and fulfilling lives. Fear is never far away; it is always on the watch for anything that might threaten our familiar and comfortable sense of self.

FEAR IS THE TRIGGER FOR MANY OF OUR ACTIONS, as well as being the root of all violence. Think about the last time you were angry and, if you look carefully, you will notice that fear was there too.

Fear can also block our actions – how many times have you intended to do something new or different, only to talk yourself out of it under the guise of being sensible?

The list of our fears is almost endless. Some basic fears that we all share are becoming ill, getting old, losing control, and dying. There are other fears, too, depending on our individual conditioning – the fear of not being liked, of not getting what we want, of disappointing people. There is the fear of humiliation, of losing our reputation and of being disapproved of. Maybe we become paralyzed between the fear of success and the fear of failure, or between wanting to be 'seen' and the fear of being 'seen'. Other fears include confrontation, intimacy and being alone.

Know Your Fear

One would think that with this much fear around we would know it quite well, but we don't. What we know well are the stories our minds keep telling us about fear. What we need to do is to get to know what fear actually is. We need to become intimate with fear.

The way to be intimate with fear is to experience it. When we feel the fear arising, we can let it reveal itself and allow it to be felt in the body. We can experience the rush of energy, the churning stomach, the pounding heartbeat, the bodily contraction and all else that fear is. We can take away the judgements and opinions about it and experience it directly.

A Tiger on the Hunt

This goes for any disturbing emotion. If we stop running from it or trying to control it in any way, then we can turn towards it and get to know its many different qualities. We come to realize that we don't have to run from it and it doesn't have to run our life. After doing this for some time, we start to see a shift. We begin to relax in the face of fear and any other strong emotion. We can see fear as being like a tiger on the hunt – it pursues us. We cannot run from it; once we start running from fear we never stop. So what we do is turn right around and face the tiger; we gently move towards the tiger and jump right into its mouth. We face the fear directly and see it for what it is – then we become free of it.

A Shift Based on Wisdom

To begin with we may find that we are still overwhelmed with fear, that its presence still paralyzes us on occasions. But if we have the courage to turn towards it time and again, the shift occurs. It is not a shift that we can bring about by brute effort. It is a shift based on wisdom, which comes from a willingness to face our own life directly. It is a shift from feeling trapped to an experience of greater freedom and happiness.

All in the Genes?

Some people seem to be naturally happy, while others are prone to depression – so is it all in the genes, and if so, are you stuck with your unhappiness? There is extensive research to suggest that genetics play a part in our level of happiness – we are conditioned by our upbringing to meet life in different ways, perhaps handle challenges more (or less) easily than the next person. However, to believe our genes have the last word on this matter is an error. Through consistent mindfulness meditation anyone can reveal their true, content nature. Freedom and happiness are not dependent on circumstances.

Thoughts and Fears

When we begin to look at fear we see that thoughts are always present – even if they are subtle thoughts hovering around in the background, they will be present. They are telling that old familiar story, telling us about dark imaginings that are sure to happen if we step beyond our comfort zone. One of the crucial things I have learned over the years is that I need to notice when I'm dwelling on fearful thoughts. I need to notice when my attention switches from whatever I am doing in the moment to obsessing about something that scares me and fills me with feelings of anxiety or dread.

Trying and Failing

When we find ourselves with issues of fear, anxiety and other disturbing emotions in our lives, it's understandable to want to be free of them. But we try to solve the issue mainly within the mental realm. In my own case, for years I felt paralyzed by fear and a lack of self-confidence. My ways of dealing with it were to condemn myself for feeling like I was, or to try to talk myself out of it. I would try analyzing it or try to rid myself of it. I would sometimes talk about it to my friends, but none of these strategies ever really worked, and I remained stuck.

A Good Look at Fear

At some point several years ago I decided that I would look at my fear and lack of self-confidence and see what they actually comprised. I noticed that they were made up of two things: bodily sensation – a churning stomach, a feeling of dread, of feeling out of control, a tight chest – and accompanying thoughts. I realized that the fear was actually a bodily response as well as a mental one. I saw that the fearful reactions were actually stored in the body, and it was with the body that I had to work them. I realized too that I had been telling myself fearful stories for decades and all those thoughts had a terrible contracting effect on my body. It's as if the body was in a constant state of fear, ready to see danger anywhere.

This is where meditation was invaluable to me. I would sit in meditation and simply experience how the body was in that moment. Instead of trying to get free of any disturbing emotions, I would allow myself to feel them. The key here, however, was to experience the sensations in the body and not to get caught up in the stories that the mind was telling me. We do not need to believe the mind. There is a greater wisdom than the thinking mind if only we allow it to reveal itself.

The Clouds Will Clear

I sat with and welcomed all the sensations of the body week after week, month after month, year after year. Sitting in this way meant that I was not actively blocking anything out of awareness. When we sit like this, with no agenda but to be open to what is there, we give space for our past to reveal itself. We will experience tears, sadness, fear, anger and whatever else is stored in our body. There may be times when we think meditation is actually making it worse, but if we have the perseverance and courage to continue, then at some point the clouds will clear and we will feel happier and less burdened by those debilitating tendencies. None of this comes about through the usual kind of effort. It happens by itself when we give space for the body to release and heal.

This is what is meant by purification. Purifying ourselves doesn't mean that we will always act with noble intentions, or that we will never have an angry thought. It means clearing away the blockages that we have accumulated from the past.

The Mind Aspect

We also need to work with the mind aspect, meaning that we need to see for ourselves the power of believed thoughts.

A female client in her mid-40s came to me with panic attacks. She had tried the usual ways of dealing with these episodes – relaxation techniques, yoga and counselling – but still they happened. Her primary response was to tense up and just wish they would go away. She often had the sense that 'something bad was going to happen' when the attacks came about. I asked where the 'bad' was when she sensed it. This took her a while to understand. Finally she saw that the 'bad' was actually thoughts in her own mind, accompanied by bodily sensations. She believed these thoughts because they had been telling her the same story for many years, which sounded convincing and in this case was the catalyst for the attacks. She started to see that the 'something bad' was actually just a story. I asked how she would feel if she didn't believe these thoughts. It was one of those 'light-bulb' moments when she realized that she wanted to believe them because they gave her a familiar sense of herself, even though it was a painful experience. This revealed to me yet again just how much we have invested in being somebody who suffers.

At least now that she has some insight into the whole affair, she knows the power of believed thoughts and her investment in being somebody who suffers. She has had the courage to continue in her awareness practice to this day, and she has come to see that to simply drop her belief in thoughts brings her relief.

All that time my client's mind had been telling her a story simply because of her conditioning. Her mind told her that something bad was going to happen. It's so easy to simply believe what the mind is telling us. It is up to us to witness the stories of the mind and stop believing them.

Embrace Fear

What is needed here is acknowledgement of the thinking that rattles through our minds constantly. If we notice we have been getting caught up in anxious thinking, we can give a moment to simply note what the mind was up to. When we see over and over that the mind is playing out the same stories (just different scenery and characters), we stop believing it. The temptation that so many people get into is to try to stop the mind and its thoughts. This we can do for a while – but they will be back, and we will carry on believing them.

So this is how we can embrace fear and all other disturbing emotions. Let the fear reveal itself with all its qualities and be vigilant regarding our thoughts. It's our belief in thoughts that keeps the whole show rolling on. At some point we will notice that fear, anger and anxiety do not bother us like they used to. We will gradually come to rest in the state of natural ease that is there waiting, and always has been.

AWARENESS PRACTICE

ON FEAR

✳

Whenever you are experiencing fear, turn towards it and give it kindness. We can see it as a part of us that is scared and needs reassurance and gentleness. Everything responds positively to kindness, so create an environment of kindness for all your emotions. Be cautious about rationalizing it away by telling yourself you know what it is about. Don't go into the story about the fear – that is not really the concern here. We are interested in the nature of fear, where we feel it, how it feels rather than the reason. You can ask yourself what it is that is so scary about this sensation. This is how we become free of fear. Give it space and let yourself experience it.

Whenever you are experiencing fear, turn towards it and give it kindness.

Less Is More

When we give our attention to the thoughts and stories surrounding difficult emotions such as fear, this generates more of that emotion. If instead we simply feel the energy in the body, we can eventually see it as just energy with a particular charge. The tendency for that energy, when left alone, is to lessen and move on.

THE WISDOM OF LONELINESS

◆

Loneliness is on the increase in nearly all Westernized countries. Our modern lifestyles are partly behind this. In our target-driven culture we can feel a constant need to be busy and productive, making it easy to neglect friendships, families and even activities that we enjoy doing for their own sake.

I HAVE HEARD LONELINESS DESCRIBED as being overwhelmed by an unbearable feeling of separation, at a very deep level. It can seem as if we are living in a glass cage and that life is happening outside of it. But actually to feel lonely and separate to some degree is natural and part of growing up. The process begins at birth. It is then we start the process of becoming individuals and, once we begin this process, we also start to seek out relationships. Once we begin to have a sense of self we also begin to have a sense of other. Where there was once an experience of oneness and safety with all of life, there is now an experience of feeling independent, disconnected and vulnerable, because if people and things are really separate from us then they can hurt us.

Separate & Connected

We move from an experience of heavenly connectedness with all of life as infants to a painful separation from life as adults. Neither of these experiences is complete because we are both separate and connected. It's a balancing act between the search for intimacy and an acceptance of separation that continues throughout our life. However smooth or difficult this passage from birth to adulthood is, there are going to be times in our lives when this process of growing up, of becoming separate individuals, feels painful, times when we feel anxious, insecure, afraid and unloved. In other words, we are going to feel lonely.

Views and Beliefs

Our painful experience as adults of feeling lonely and cut off from life is because we don't see life clearly. This is because we have beliefs that we don't realize we have. We have beliefs and views about ourselves that are basically untrue and which we have not investigated. We may have been told that we are ugly, that nobody likes us, that we are useless and will never amount to anything. These words may have actually been said or we may have just picked up the 'silent' message over the years of growing up. These views and beliefs get massaged into our being and we accept them for who we are.

The Experience of Loneliness

Our most basic belief is that we exist separate from life – 'I exist and life is something that happens to me.' This belief is the primary cause of the experience of loneliness. Friendships and intimate relationships are some of the most joyful and satisfying experiences each of us can have, but they will not ease the existential experience of feeling separate and alone. Some of the loneliest of people have busy jobs and very active social lives, and can appear to be doing very well. Often, however, an unease about life exists underneath, a loneliness that they are scared to let out of its corner for fear of being devoured by it. So down in the corner it stays and rears its little head in moments of quiet, only to be shoved back again when the anxious tremble begins. We keep it hidden because we don't know how to face up to this underlying anxiety about our lives. We keep ourselves busy. At least the busy life we have created is something that is known to us, it gives us a sense of security, a notion of who we are and how we are, which gives us a feeling of safety. But we need to heal this disconnection, to experience the loneliness we run from.

Listen to the Message

Most of us would like loneliness to leave us alone. We would like to be free of it once and for all. However, it is impossible to rid ourselves of these experiences and if we try to it is absolutely certain that we will suffer more distress as a consequence, because to try to rid ourselves of something within us is an act of violence. If we could eliminate it, where would it go? If we engage in this approach we succeed only in demonizing it even more.

The experience of loneliness is telling us something – there is wisdom there, if we know how to listen to its message. If we feel disconnected from life, we are disconnected from ourselves. This means we are out of touch with our deeper feelings, and getting in touch with our deeper feelings is what mindfulness is about. It is showing us where our vision is limited. It is pointing to the fact that we are not connected to our true nature, which is precisely why we feel disconnected.

Intimacy with Life

Our true nature is not a thing we can grasp or understand intellectually, but an experience of ease and spaciousness that includes all of life. Our true nature *is* our connection with all and everything. When we open to our deeper nature, our experience is then one of intimacy with life. The *little me*, the self-image that exists in the head, is seen for what it is, a story we have been telling ourselves all our life. The *little me* is the experience of loneliness because it is only interested in its own survival, so creates stories about itself which we believe as absolutely true. It doesn't matter if the stories are pleasant or unpleasant, what matters is that the *little me* exists independently from everything and everybody else.

Being Comfortable with the Intolerable

Through mindfulness, we can increase our ability to experience and become comfortable with those aspects that we find intolerable. Often we demonize the experience of loneliness, leading to conflict within ourselves. We may say to ourselves things like, 'I hate this loneliness, I know I'm going to feel lonely for ever. Or 'Why me, why should this happen to me?' But these views and opinions just tie the knot of loneliness ever tighter. I did this myself for years with loneliness. I hated it. I hated myself for feeling lonely and afraid and saw myself as weak because of it. I tried many strategies to eliminate loneliness from my life and failed miserably. I would pretend it wasn't there and fake confidence and sociability. But it sat there like a weight on my shoulders, only occasionally easing, but soon returning seemingly out of nowhere.

An Unexpected Guide

It was only when I stopped running away from it that things started to change. Instead of indulging all the judgements and opinions about the experience, I started to welcome it and observe it. I began to experience the sensation of loneliness in my body. I discovered that I wasn't so afraid of it – this was wonderful. What I also observed was that through mindfulness practice I was *feeling* more in my life – more anger, more joy, more desire, more pleasure. I was feeling more alive. I had more energy. The experience of loneliness seemed to evaporate without me trying to do anything to it or with it. This illustrated to me yet again the power of awareness and the wisdom of loneliness itself to guide me back to my own direct experience. I realized that loneliness was a symbol and the symbol was pointing out to me that I was disconnected from my own emotional life.

An Act of Love

To welcome loneliness or any other difficult experience in this way is an act of love. When we are sitting in meditation we need to be willing to feel our bodily sensations. Feeling these sensations allows all those 'unacceptable' feelings that have been 'frozen out' of awareness to begin to dissolve and start to flow again. Awareness is like the sun – if we put a block of ice in the sun, after a little while it dissolves back into its original nature, which is flowing water. Similarly, when we bring mindfulness to our bodies we dissolve and release all those stuck energies, which are then free to flow again. It may be uncomfortable for a while, but with kindness and perseverance the rewards always come.

Free of Loneliness

The only way to be free of loneliness is to stop avoiding it. We can take away the label of *loneliness* and be mindful of its energy. For example, when I was leading a meditation retreat once a woman spoke out and said, 'I'm bored, whenever I sit for long periods I just get bored.' I asked her how she knew it was boredom. Then I suggested that she take away the label 'boredom' and simply be with the experience itself. Later that day she spoke again. 'I have realized that boredom is a story I have been telling myself. It is a label I have given an experience and, when I take away the label of boredom, I am not bored. I don't know what it is, it is something, but it's not boredom.' She had realized something profound, that she experienced life not directly, but filtered through her thoughts. I encouraged her then to be with this 'something'. To give it space, to let it breathe and move and dance, let it crawl or sing or cry. I suggested she give it room to be exactly what it wants to be. We can do this with what we label *loneliness*. Take away the label that you have given it for years and let it be. No need to try to eliminate it, to try to change it or have opinions

The only way to be free of
loneliness is to stop avoiding it.
We can take away the label of loneliness
and be mindful of its energy.

about it. Leave it alone and let it be felt. Allow it to move through you, let it take whatever form it wants to take. Observe where you feel it, notice how it feels. Give it room to lie down or to curl up and weep. Be gentle, kind and patient. Let it reveal itself to you.

AWARENESS PRACTICE
ON LONELINESS

✳

Bring the experience of loneliness to mind. Observe how it makes you feel. Do you want to get rid of it? Do you feel resistant to welcoming it? If so, welcome these feelings. Observe where you feel it and what it feels like. Observe its qualities, its shape; does it have a colour? Be aware of the thoughts around the whole issue.

When we observe in this way we objectify it and realize that we are not the loneliness. We can say that a part of us feels lonely, but that is not the whole of us.

Then, moving on, ask yourself, 'What proof do I have that I am lonely, apart from the thoughts and bodily sensations? If I drop the story that I am lonely, what is left?'

HAPPINESS IN A WORLD OF WANTS

◆

Pursuit of the material things of this world has reached a point of absurdity — and we know it. Materialism is the new religion, but many of us are now growing tired of working harder to buy more of the things we only think we want. So why do we do it?

WHEN WE ARE OUT OF TOUCH with our true nature, out of touch with our innate joy of life, we experience ourselves as lacking something, and if we don't realize our true nature, we always will. Our attitude then is of wanting something to feel complete. Wanting to feel complete or happy is what lies at the root of all human activity, even though we may not realize it. We try desperately to fill this sense of lack with the things and activities of this world.

Beings with Desire

As humans we are beings with desire, but acquiring the objects that we desire does not lead to the satisfaction we hope for, apart from a brief afterglow; then desire fires up again and we are looking for the next fix. All of us are addicts; we just crave different objects — some, it must be said, less harmful than others.

At some point in our lives we may come to the point of disillusionment with gross materialism, with treading endlessly on the wheel of wanting, and I am often asked if renunciation is the way forward. The assumption then is that if acquiring all these things is not making me happy, I will stop. This approach can work, but more often than not it doesn't. This way normally leads to repression of our desires and is not advised. Desire is energy and it cannot be manipulated or stopped any more than the weather can. Desire is our life force and needs to be treated that way, and to deny or repress it can lead to serious illness.

How Desire Manifests

There are three ways that desire can play out in our lives. The first is that we get overwhelmed with wanting: wanting things, people's approval, security, money and reputation. The second way is that we repress and deny our desire and we can become rather anaemic and even ill. The third way – what we can call the middle way – is one of beginning to observe desire. We don't entertain any opinions and judgements about it, but just experience it and pay attention to it, and this is the way of mindfulness.

Being Mindful of Desire

Awareness doesn't have criticisms or views about how we live our lives, it just simply heals them. Normally when we desire something our attention goes towards the object of that desire. For example, if I desire a new mobile phone (and it must be said I already have a perfectly good one), instead of just plunging in head first and getting a new one, I can instead be mindful of the desire. I can ask myself what the desire actually feels like. Where do I feel the desire? I can notice also the story around the whole issue. I can observe all the rationalizations that pass through my mind to convince me I need it. Initially this can be a difficult thing to do, as the habit of acquiring what I want is very strong. But that is my practice, that is how mindfulness helps me to release the grip that desire and wanting have over me. Whether I get the new phone or not is secondary. The point is that I have started to be mindful of the whole process. Through awareness I begin to see the difference between wanting things to feel better and the healthy desire to have a new phone.

The Joy of Being

We are constantly wanting and desiring because we are out of touch with our source of joy. The joy that I am talking about is the joy of being – it is our birthright. It is not something that can be given or taken away by anybody. As a consequence, we settle for crumbs of comfort that we are being told we need in order to be happy. When we touch and open to this joy of being, we want for nothing, but enjoy everything, even new mobile phones. We don't have to deny ourselves the things of the world, but we are not dependent on them for our happiness either. We can be happy with them or without them. They don't own us any more, we own them.

I am already that which I seek. Whatever I seek or think I want, however long the shopping list may be, all my desires are only a reflection of my longing to come home. And home is oneness, home is my original nature. It is right here, simply in what is. There is nowhere else I have to go, and nothing else I have to become.

FROM 'THE OPEN SECRET' BY TONY PARSONS
OPEN SECRET PUBLISHING, 2000

Abiding in the Present

Through mindfulness meditation we see how much we live in anticipation of what is to come. This is not living in the present, and to be happy we need to live in the present. Living in the present doesn't mean we don't think about the future or which phone to buy, but means that it is done without anxiety and anticipation. Through awareness practice, the balance changes from living mainly in anticipation of the future and trying to be present, to abiding in the present and being able to think about the future, or not. We are not endlessly worrying about it, we are content, happy and joyful.

Relationship to Money

To be without certain material possessions can be frightening, because it is how many of us find some self-worth. When it comes to money itself, it is even stronger. It is good to know our relationship to money. Maybe we are constantly frightened of having none, or we just fritter it away on things we don't need so we can avoid uncomfortable feelings. It is good to bring the whole issue of money into our spiritual lives. Money is so mundane, but spirituality, if it is to make a difference, we must include everything mundane. Often we seek identity in money – having lots of it can make us feel powerful and having little can be scary. If we look to money to feel good about ourselves, we are on an endless and unsatisfying journey – the more we get, the more we want. If having lots of money led to contentment, then pursuing it would be understandable, but how much is enough? Amassing more and more money is the focus of many people's lives, but has it led to happiness that is not dependent on money itself? The answer, if we are honest, is no. Money, just like everything in life, is uncertain and we worry that we may lose it.

Observe & Understand

When we take up mindfulness meditation we don't oppose anything, not even money and materialism. The practice of mindfulness is to observe and understand how we are, not to interfere with how we are. Mindfulness has nothing to do with opinions, views and criticisms about ourselves, but is an observing of everything about us, including those opinions, views and criticisms. With awareness, our interest needs to be with what is happening now, even if that is a stampede of anxious thoughts about the future. If there is no awareness of these thoughts they will generate emotion and, before you know it, you will be in the shop buying your new shoes or feeling depressed because you cannot afford them.

◆

Spiritual practice must include everything, even the temporal world of money. We may imagine that, spiritual practitioners that we are, finances are not worthy of our consideration; yet these issues make an especially rich field for practice. Money issues are rarely about money. Observe your beliefs and behaviours around money – try to see them with clarity and precision. Then bring awareness to the well of emotion out of which your beliefs and behaviours arise. You may discover that behind most financial insecurity is the terror of losing control or feeling helpless. Honestly facing this fear is the price we pay to be free.

FROM 'SAYING YES TO LIFE (EVEN THE HARD PARTS)' BY EZRA BAYDA
WISDOM PUBLICATIONS, 2005

◆

Lost in Doing

Materialism isn't only about valuing things, but is a way of life. It's about filling our life with doing things as well as consuming things. It seems that doing nothing or idling is frowned upon as wasting time, but as one Zen master said, 'Busyness is the height of laziness.' We don't want to stop the busyness for fear that we will actually experience what is going on inside us. To stop and be still or to pay attention to how we are can be very uncomfortable and even shocking at first. The vast majority of people who come on my retreats are tired of the madness that has become their lives. It often takes a few days to 'come around' out of the 'haze of activity', but when they do it's a great relief and they are often reluctant to go back to their normal lives, and want to make changes. When we are lost in 'doing', we lose touch with our innate ability to just be. We are out of balance. When we can idle and rest in 'being', we are then in a position to appreciate the moment, but in our march towards building a future we miss the very joy that is right there in each footstep. I am not advocating that we all give up the world and sit around all day, far from it. However, when our activity is not balanced by our own ability to be still, we suffer as a consequence.

The Key to Contentment

Awareness in the form of mindfulness is the key to a contented life. Through mindfulness we pay attention to the surge of thoughts and bodily sensations that drive us to be busy. Through mindfulness we pay attention to that energy that keeps us busy. What we find, if we are curious enough, is a very subtle but very real 'insecure tremble' or deep anxiety about our lives. We can spend all our lives running from this 'insecure tremble', because we are scared to face it. However, if we fail to turn towards and become comfortable with this sense of anxiety it will run our lives and leave us exhausted in the process. It is this underlying deep anxiety that we need to welcome and observe. Welcome it and let it be felt and experienced. Notice what it feels like, observe where you experience it, and give it space to breathe. Treat it kindly and over time you will experience a sense of ease enter into your life. Welcome everything about yourself, the good, the bad and the ugly. It is the only way that our lives truly heal. It is the only way that the inner 'enemies' transform into friends and allies that accompany us in harmony on our journey.

I Have Enough

When I watch sport or celebrity shows on TV, it seems that everybody is wanting everything. It is a very 'me'-oriented world, where this me cannot get enough. This rampant materialism is not good for us. To be emotionally healthy we must be without some of the things we want. If we just get everything we want, then we never have to show self-control. Through the practice of mindfulness and self-control we cease being slaves to materialism and our wants and we learn the meaning of three beautiful words – I HAVE ENOUGH.

AWARENESS PRACTICE

ON DESIRE

❋

Think of something that you want – a phone, a car, a holiday, shouldn't be difficult. Observe the object of your desire in your mind's eye. Be aware of its features – its shape, colour, size. Imagine what you could do with it and how it would make you feel to possess it or do it. Observe how thinking about it increases the desire for it.

Now turn your attention to the desire itself. Notice where you feel it, observe the shape of the desire – it doesn't matter if you cannot be accurate here. Be mindful of the qualities of the desire itself. We are not trying to do anything with desire, but are just looking and being aware of it. Take a step back, as it were, and observe the desire. Give it space and breathe.

This is how we create inner spaciousness, which brings with it an ease and well-being that are not dependent on getting everything we want.

DON'T WORRY ABOUT A THING

◆

Most of us seem to be under the impression that we can change the world merely by thinking about it — we must believe that, or why would we spend so much time worrying? But thinking endlessly doesn't change anything — all that happens is that we end up tense and miserable.

I F A FRIEND OR LOVED ONE IS LATE, does your mind go over and over the same old thoughts, telling the same old story? Maybe the story is that they have had an accident, or that they don't care for you any more.

If we are worrying over something, maybe giving a public talk in a few days' time, or going for an interview, we obsess about it in the mistaken belief that this will make a positive difference, but we can of course only do what needs to be done – prepare for the talk – and no more.

Obsessing or worrying about something serves only one purpose – to leave us agitated and unhappy, in a state of perpetual unease and distress, and far less efficient at doing whatever it is that needs doing.

Obsessing or worrying about something leave us agitated and unhappy.

Walking down the road in the evening, the birds are singing; little window-boxes have little flowers coming out of them; the children may be playing out in the street. There are so many delightful and wonderful things but when we are pre-occupied we see very little. Most of our life is spent asleep because we are doing the very important work of anaesthetizing ourselves. This is what worry is: addiction to thought, to repetitive thought, it is a way of making yourself stupid. Half an hour of worry is the same as hitting yourself with a hammer! If somebody said, 'Okay, I'll save you time, let me hit you with a hammer,' you'd say, 'No! No! I prefer to do it myself!'

JAMES LOW (EVENING TALK AT THE STADTRAUM IN COLOGNE),
GERMANY, 27 APRIL 2005

Worry or Concern?

You may think that to worry about someone or something is an indication that you care, but there is a difference between worry and concern. It comes down to a definition of terms, and to be worried is very different to being concerned. Worry has an obsessive tendency to it; you may find yourself going over the same thoughts again and again. Worry is the mind running the emotions, and if the emotions are swirling around out of control, then it is difficult to be objective. It either paralyzes you or you react to the worrisome thoughts and barge in without awareness. It is difficult to stop worrying, but you can be aware of it. Let go of believing in thinking and you will know how to act. How often do you think yourself into believing something bad is going to happen, only to later realize it was all in your mind? Being concerned, on the other hand, still leaves you with the mental space to foresee something that may happen and be prepared for it, if necessary; it may spur you into positive action.

AWARENESS PRACTICE

ON WORRY

❋

Worry is thought. It is thinking about something that may or may not happen in the future. But where is the future when you are not thinking about it?

Sit quietly. Can you find the future without thinking, or visualizing it? When you are not thinking or visualizing in any way, where is the future?

When it is seen clearly that the past and the future are thought-created, you arrive naturally without effort in the present – and the present moment is the only place we can be truly happy. When we are present we know how to act for the benefit of all concerned.

No Blame

I never blame myself when I'm not hitting the ball. I
just blame the bat, and if it continues, I change bats.
After all, if I know it isn't my fault that I'm
not hitting, then how can I get mad at myself.

ANONYMOUS AMERICAN BASEBALL PLAYER

*When things and people are not how we want them to be, it is so very
easy to slip into a blaming behaviour pattern. Blaming others is a
way of deflecting attention away from where it needs to be, and that
is towards the emotion behind the blaming.*

IT IS NOT ABOUT BLAMING OURSELVES EITHER, as that is just
another way of avoiding what is really going on. Often we
will blame others for making us feel bad. It may be anger, sadness, hurt, humiliation or jealousy. Getting into blaming at
this point is a way of not owning up to our own pain, a way of
continuing to avoid the underlying hurt and fear that we have
spent years trying to avoid. We have all sorts of strategies to
avoid this pain; overdrinking, overeating, too much televi-
sion, trying to be successful, drugs, keeping busy, not engaging
with life, being nice, people-pleasing. It is good to know
which strategies are our favourites. The assumption when we
are blaming is that if the other person stops their behaviour,
or if they change, then we will be OK.

A woman went to the doctor and asked, 'Doctor, I have a terrible head-ache, could you give me something for it?' 'Of course, my dear. Sit down, I just want to ask you a few questions,' the doctor replied. After he had finished the doctor said, 'I'm going to give you these tablets and I want you to give them to your husband.' 'Oh, thank you, doctor,' replied the woman, 'I feel better already.'

We often think it's other people who need to take the medicine, who need to change. Trying to change other people in this way actually makes no real difference to us. It just means we put off looking at our own pain a little longer. If others do change (and that of course may be necessary sometimes if there is gross behaviour), we still have not healed our own sensitive issues. They will lie there until the next time someone criticizes us, or challenges us.

The Mechanics of Blame

Let's look at what happens when we get into blaming. Say a loved one criticizes us and we are left feeling angry. What often happens is that we go on the attack; we may verbally lash out at them, blaming them for how we feel. We may be certain that they are to blame for how we feel. But if we take a closer look at what is actually happening in the moment – which is the last thing we want to do – we will find we are lost in thinking. If we are willing to ask ourselves, 'What's going on right now?', we will find that it is we who are creating the anger. It is the belief in the thoughts that is creating the anger and generating more of it. Again, if we are willing to pay attention we see that blaming is simply a defence mechanism, a defence against feeling our own vulnerability, pain and unhappiness. We lash out so that we can get others to deal with their stuff while we can feel a victim.

What we need to do is to experience our own feelings of anger. If we are willing to ask, 'What's happening right now?', we will see that we are lost in a story about how bad the other person is. If we are willing to leave the story and come back to the body we will experience the physical effects of anger. If we can remain curious we may notice that behind the anger is another emotion – fear or hurt. We need to learn to stay with the felt experience of this in the body. This is the way to heal our long-held wounds.

What We Feel, We Heal

On retreat I quite often say, 'What we feel, we heal.' Often someone will respond that they feel a lot and they don't seem to be healing at all. What's happening here is that, although there is a lot of feeling going on, there is also the telling of the story about it in their mind. Staying with the storyline doesn't heal our pain, but creates more. Thinking of course has its place in our life, but it will never lead us to freedom and happiness; in fact, quite often it keeps us stuck where we are, in our own self-centred view of the world.

Kindly Attention

Once a woman who felt stuck in her life came to see me. She had developed a bad stomach, and though doctors and homeopaths tried to help, they made little difference. While sitting with her one day I asked her to take her attention to her stomach, which was upset. I asked her to simply give her stomach some kindly attention. She sat there for a few minutes, then I asked her to sense what her stomach needed from her. She sat there curiously listening to her stomach, and then the response came. The response jolted her and brought tears to her eyes...her stomach asked her to stop thinking about it so much. It wanted to be left alone to get on with its work. She realized that all the thinking about her stomach was actually the primary reason it was not well. She told me that almost all of the waking day she was wondering how her stomach was. Was it better than yesterday? Was it feeling OK?

> *It is experiencing our fear, anger, hurt, grief and anxiety directly in the moment that leads to their healing.*

Take the Opportunity...

It is experiencing our fear, anger, hurt, grief and anxiety directly in the moment that leads to their healing, not endlessly thinking about them.

So next time you find yourself lost in blaming, use it as an opportunity to see what you are defending. You can guarantee that behind the blaming will be hurt and fear, and this is where we need to take our attention if we want to be free and happy.

Work in Progress

Do we need to work at happiness throughout our lives? The answer to that is both yes and no. We need to be vigilant as to when we are 'doing unhappiness', or being overwhelmed by our fears and anxieties, as we will for a good while. As we practise, however, we open up more and more to our deeper nature, which is happiness itself, and once we start to taste this we are never quite the same again, and there is something in us that knows that we can trust in this.

AWARENESS PRACTICE

ON BLAMING

❋

Next time you find yourself blaming someone, look for the feeling behind the blame and you will find hurt. Feel the hurt, comfort it, and let it be as it is without interfering in any way. Notice how eventually it fades away into nothing if left alone and not sustained by thinking. However, when we are experiencing it, our motive isn't to eliminate it, but to be with it – an important point. Give up the agenda of trying to change or rid yourself of uncomfortable feelings.

CHAPTER FIVE

WAKING UP

*This book casts aside all our preconceived ideas
about happiness — what it is, what it isn't, and why
searching outside ourselves for happiness is futile,
both because we won't find it and because we don't
need to. We already have it, and need only to learn how
to connect with it through mindful meditation. In this
chapter we remind ourselves of the ultimate aim of the
work we've done so far — waking up to life — and
finish with the loving-kindness meditation that
is at the heart of the Buddhist tradition
of compassion for all.*

A man who had been practising meditation for many years, and who'd experienced a host of cosmic experiences, went to a famous master for confirmation of his spiritual achievement. The master said, 'Sit down, I'd like to ask you a few questions first.'

'Who are you?' asked the master.

'My name is William,' replied the man.

'I didn't ask your name, but who you are,' said the master.

'I'm American,' replied the man.

'I didn't ask your nationality, but who you are,' replied the master.

'I'm a husband and father of two sons.'

'I didn't ask whether you are a father or not, but who you are.'

'I'm an architect.'

'I didn't ask what your profession is, but who you are.'

'I'm a Buddhist.' And on and on it went.

'Who are you?'

'In my spare time I help the poor and needy.'

'I didn't ask about your spare time, but who you are.'

'I'm a meditator.'

This went on and on and, no matter how many times he was asked, he couldn't see the master's point.

The master finally said, 'When you know your appearance from who you really are, come back.'

HEART OF THE MATTER

◆

What is the ultimate purpose of meditation, of spiritual practice?
It is to wake up to who we really are and to free ourselves from
suffering. This is the heart of the matter; it's what all those hours of
meditation and being aware are really about.

IT'S WHAT THE BUDDHA AND CHRIST and all the other great
spiritual teachers were pointing to. For a few rare individuals,
this waking up to who they are happens spontaneously.
Their true nature (Buddha nature, God, The Beloved; whatever we wish to call it) bursts forth and shows itself for what
it really is – this seemingly without any effort on the individual's part. However, for most of us who want to wake up,
who want to be free and happy, it is not so simple. We need
to put in some effort, develop some kind of intelligent
spiritual practice – we need to engage in some form of meditation. We need to learn the art of being aware, because it is
through awareness that we free ourselves from the misery
that can otherwise dictate our lives.

Our Sense of Self

The root of our suffering, as we have seen, is a sense of self,
separate from all the other selves out there. Over the years
of growing up and becoming an adult, we build an identity
out of this sense of self, like the man in the story opposite.

In doing so, we lose contact with our true nature. This sense of self, which in some cases can be very constricted, then becomes our prison. At this point we try to decorate the prison, to make it as cosy as possible and a nice place to live in. This is the area of self-improvement.

Awareness practice (meditation) allows us to see what imprisons us, to study the walls of the prison and find a way out of it completely. Never mind tinkering with the place, never mind repainting the walls, never mind putting up some fancy new curtains, or polishing the furniture; it's about escaping the prison altogether.

A State of Confusion

What we don't realize is that we are already happy and free, but we don't *experience* it because our minds are confused. We spend nearly all our time preoccupied by the machinations and demands of the ego, of the sense of this separate *me*. This makes us feel both real and very important – but it is also the root cause of all our suffering and unhappiness.

Of course we are separate too and that is not to be denied. But this experience of our self as separate from others is in some cases so strong and habitual that we may not even begin to think that the reality of the situation could be different. (Of course, if you're reading this then you have at least an awareness that there's more to life than this sense of separation, than being in prison.)

Setting Ourselves Free

The way out of the prison is not to deny that we are separate individuals; rather, it's understanding that the experience of separation is not the whole picture. As well as experiencing the diversity of life, experiencing the difference between us, we need to see the underlying unity too.

How is this realized? How do we free ourselves from this self-made prison? The answer is that we don't need to do anything, we don't need to add anything on to who we are. We don't need to develop any special qualities, or engage in trying endlessly to change ourselves into somebody else – we are complete as we are. We do, however, need to be aware of the thinking mind that is running the show, and to observe the endless games of our slippery minds.

The Nature of the Self

The self, the sense of *me*, has ways of reinforcing itself. One way is through judging others. When we judge others we feel either superior or inferior; either way there's a strong sense of *me* there, as separate from other people. What we judge that we cannot understand, we distance ourselves from.

Another way the self reinforces itself is through comparison. The self cannot see differences without comparing as better or worse, again reinforcing itself as different.

The self doesn't like uncertainty. It would rather create a story that causes us to suffer than be in a space of unknowing.

The self constantly needs to be affirmed. It needs approval. It needs its fix of appreciation and approval, and to be noticed in a good light.

Notice Your Self

During the day, notice how many times you want attention, how many times you want to be seen to be special in some way. Notice your assumptions about others and life in general. Notice how you act to please others, quite often at the expense of what you really want to do. Notice when you want to say no, but end up saying yes instead. A sign that you are waking up is being able to say no.

Notice what it feels like the next time you are praised or criticized. The elation we feel when praised is setting us up for feeling depressed when criticized. Notice how much we blame others for how we feel.

These are all ways in which we give our power away and let other people dictate how we feel. Wouldn't it be wonderful to be free and not constantly seek approval from others? Wouldn't it be wonderful to not constantly seek others' permission to feel OK about who and how we are?

A Natural Change

Observe all this as non-judgementally as possible. If you do judge, then that too can simply be noticed. Observe all this without trying to change anything at all about yourself.

Instead of trying to change your experience into what you think it should be, simply understand it as it is. Do this and watch the change in you occur quite naturally; change will happen through awareness.

As you pay attention in this way you will notice that all the demands of the ego, all the judging and blaming begin to weaken. You will find yourself experiencing more peace, more freedom and greater happiness. You will find yourself relaxing into the openness that is your true nature – not because you have added anything, or because you have 'acquired' happiness (it cannot be acquired), but because that which causes suffering has started to fall away.

When we're not caught up with the screaming ego and we see the self for what it is, we discover freedom and happiness, and we see that they were there all the time.

AWARENESS PRACTICE

ON THE SPACE BETWEEN THOUGHTS

❋

Normally when we meditate we are aware of thoughts, feelings and emotions, which can be called objects of awareness. For this awareness practice, notice the gaps between thoughts when meditating. Notice the space within which all experiences happen. Notice the container (awareness) and not just the contents of awareness. This helps us weaken our attachments to thoughts and feelings, leading to inner spaciousness.

LETTING GO OF EVERYTHING

We can see meditation as a continuous process of letting go. We let go of the bundle of lifelong habits that cause us suffering and unhappiness. We let go of all the limiting views that lead us to live a small, fearful and cramped life. In a word, we let go of the self.

So how do we let go? As an example, let's look at how we let go and relax when we meditate. When we sit we tune into the felt experience of the body. As we do this we sense how the body is. We may see that we are a little agitated, maybe a little tense. We feel how we are and we accept how we are. We don't try to relax, but allow everything to be simply as it is. We let go of trying to be different from how we are, which leads to greater relaxation.

This is the essence of meditation: nothing special at all. Within this felt experience of the body we allow whatever comes into awareness to simply be and to move on. Our work isn't to interfere or to try to change it, but to observe it and let go and relax. Relaxation can't be forced; it is a natural result of letting go of tension and contraction.

Just Observe

As you sit, you will notice that some of your senses are being activated. You may notice sounds, or certain smells; all you need do is notice and let them go.

It is the same with any bodily sensations, too, whether fear, anxiety, sadness, joy or raging ecstasy – simply observe them, and let them go. By observing, I mean feeling them just as they are and not believing our opinions about them.

At times, perhaps quite a lot of the time, you may notice lots of mental chattering, lots of thoughts. You may observe, for instance, that you have been lost in an imaginary conversation – so you notice, let go and come back to the felt experience of the body.

Or you may observe that you were lost in planning the future – notice that too, and return awareness to the body. When you realize that you are lost in thought, take a moment to notice that, label it 'thinking', then simply let go and come back to your felt experience of the moment. No judgement or condemnation is necessary.

Do this over and over again with gentleness and patience. Observe, observe, observe – let go, let go, let go.

Feel It in Your Bones

Noticing our thoughts allows us to see where we are holding on. For instance, we may realize that there are resentful thoughts present. Or we may see that we are complaining about something to ourselves, but all we need do is notice this tendency of the mind to hold on and let it pass. Once we see for ourselves that the obsessive mind serves no purpose but to cause suffering, letting go will happen more and more easily.

Actually, we won't be able to stop it. This process needs to be done over and over again until we know it in our bones.

As we let go of thought we come back into the felt presence of the body and the breath. We simply let go into the aliveness of the body. We don't let go into thinking about the body, or an image of the body, but the feeling of the body.

The Illusion of Problems

As we practise in this way we may encounter fear and resistance. This is because we are letting go of our very own intimate sense of self, the ego. The ego is only interested in its own survival and that means stirring up fears and anxieties about the future. It wants to think about all the things that are (not) going to happen, and all the problems we (don't) have, just to keep us from reality, just to keep us from being present with life as it is. I'm reminded of a saying by that great American Mark Twain, 'I'm an old man, I've had many problems, most of them didn't happen.' The ego will create the illusion of problems where there aren't any just to keep us restless and unhappy, because that's what it's familiar with.

Stick with It…

If we persevere in letting go in this way, then after a time a shift takes place, a gradual shift, but one that has enormous benefits. The shift is from identification with ego, with thoughts, with the stories that we tell ourselves, to one of identification with awareness itself, with spaciousness itself. In other words, we stop believing the constantly chattering mind with all its fears and anxieties and judgements and begin to dwell in the natural openness and spaciousness of our true nature. It is the constant belief in thoughts that keeps them proliferating, and drives many of us to exhaustion and some of us almost to madness.

It's wonderful when we start to see that meditation isn't about adding anything on to ourselves or endlessly trying to change ourselves – it is simply about observing all the ways that we cause our own suffering, and there are many. As we observe ourselves in this way, both on the meditation cushion and in everyday life, we realize that we were already free and happy and that all the ways we tried to acquire happiness were just getting in the way.

◆

I sometimes quite happily do nothing! But when
I'm doing nothing, I don't mean 'not doing anything'!
Not sort of sitting there in a slightly negative mood feeling
that you're not doing anything but maybe you ought to be
doing something. If there is something to be done, well,
of course, do it! But if there is nothing to be done, well,
positively enjoy that state of not doing anything!

'IN PEACE IS A FIRE' BY SANGHARAKSHITA
WINDHORSE PUBLICATIONS, 1995

◆

AWARENESS PRACTICE
ON LETTING GO
❋

Practise letting go in your life. Start with the small things. Notice when you want to repeat a pleasurable experience. For example, be aware of how you want to hold on to a lovely evening out with a friend. Nothing wrong with that in itself and it's understandable, but simply notice without judgement. Observe how you want to grasp on to a pleasurable experience in meditation.

Observe how you hold on to views about your self and others. How you get defensive when someone challenges you. Be aware of your thoughts when meditating and let them go. Don't hold on to anything. Let go, let go, let go!

I'm reminded of a saying by Mark Twain, 'I'm an old man, I've had many problems, most of them didn't happen.'

WHO ARE YOU – REALLY?

◆

All the misery on this planet arises due to our
personalized sense of 'me' or 'us'. That covers up the
essence of who you are. When you are unaware of that
inner essence, in the end you always create misery. It's as
simple as that. When you don't know who you are, you
create a mind-made self as a substitute for your beautiful
divine being and cling to that fearful and needy self.

FROM 'STILLNESS SPEAKS: WHISPERS OF NOW' BY ECKHART TOLLE
HODDER MOBIUS, 2003

◆

*People often say that this or that person has not yet 'found himself'.
But the self is not something one finds, it is something one creates.
We take up careers, get into relationships, adopt views and beliefs,
and these become our identities – but they are not who we are.*

WE ALL EXPERIENCE DISTRESS, anxiety, frustration and
pain about our lives and ourselves. And most of us
have a similar response to this situation, and normally that
response is that we don't know what to do about it. Some
common ways of coping are to set about finding our perfect
partner to make it all right for us. We may seek promotion
and find solace in this new-found status. We may take to
drowning ourselves in overwork in order to avoid having to
face up to our often painful experience.

A Better Person

One thing we are all deceived about is that we think we have to do something to get out of what at times seems an unbearable situation. It often takes the form of trying to improve ourselves and become a 'better' person. This is an understandable, though worthless task.

Ask yourself – has trying to become a better person ever led to fulfilment, apart from momentary satisfaction? Has anything of the external world ever led you to peace?

The answer, if you are honest, will be no, it hasn't. Then why do we persist in this same old way? We persist because of a mistaken belief that we are our thoughts and the image that these thoughts conjure up. The mind throws up stories about ourselves and life and we mistakenly believe that if we can fulfil these stories, then all will be well. It's a hopeless task, leaving us exhausted and bereft of meaning.

We mistakenly think that we need to improve ourselves and our life somehow in order to be happy and find the peace we are looking for. To do this we turn to the familiar world of thoughts and striving for a different future that will deliver the elusive something, which we think will make us happy.

Something of Value

This belief in the stories the mind creates is the cause of our existential distress. The mind hoodwinks us into thinking it has the answer to our problem, when it is the problem itself, or rather, it is our mistaken belief in the thoughts, that is the problem. We trust in thoughts because this is the only thing we know. We don't experience anything much beyond thought because we are mesmerized by the thinking process. But if we are willing to accept that maybe there is 'something of value' beyond our thoughts, then we are at the beginning of a new and profound discovery of who we really are.

Watch Your Thoughts, Watch Your Feelings

If we can sit and watch our thoughts, after a while it may dawn on us that there is something watching the thoughts. So by logical conclusion we can see, at least intellectually, that we are not our thoughts. The thoughts come and go, but the awareness of them remains. Even when we are lost in thinking, when 'we' return there is still a knowing of the thoughts.

If we sit and feel the feelings of the body come and go, after a while we may realize that there is something knowing the feelings. We see that there is something aware of the feelings. What normally happens is that we identify with our feelings and want to turn them into nice feelings. We may think that turning the feelings into good feelings is what meditation and spiritual practice are about. If I can feel good and only have nice thoughts and feelings, then all will be well.

But if we pay attention we can see that if feelings, just like thoughts, come and go, but the awareness of them remains, then maybe we are not merely our feelings.

*We take all the stories
of the mind and believe the
story is who we are.*

Attachment to Labels

It is the same with self-identities, or 'labels' – I am a doctor, I am a communist, I am a Conservative, I am a Christian, and so on. We attach to our labels and if anyone challenges them, then heaven help them.

If we are willing to look, we can see that there is something behind all the thinking, feelings and beliefs we hold so dearly. That something is our true and happier nature, which can be so easily overlooked because we are hypnotized by the mind and all its agitated thinking. We take all the stories of the mind and believe the story is who we are.

It's like having a blackboard and filling some of it in with chalk marks. All we really see are the chalk marks and not the space in between. We easily get attached to objects and neglect the space around them. We get so carried away with our thinking (which is mostly about ourselves) that we forget the space in which it all appears.

AWARENESS PRACTICE

ON SELF-IDENTITY

✳

Take your time doing the following exercises. Allow a few minutes for each one. If you experience any discomfort or fear doing these exercises, then allow that to be the object of awareness. Notice where you feel it and what it really feels like. It is only the small 'I' wanting to stay in control.

Ask yourself – am I the body?

The body is changing moment by moment. Every seven years it is a completely new body through the dying and birth of cells. The body is 'loaned' from the earth, it is made up of earth, water, fire (heat) and air and all these elements are 'given' back at our death.

Ask yourself – am I my thoughts?

If you were your thoughts, how could you observe them?

If you were your thoughts, wouldn't you choose only to think positive ones? Thoughts are not who you are, they arise and pass away without any effort on your part. Look for the thinker of the thoughts.

Ask yourself – am I my feelings?

Feelings are so transient, so uncertain; they come and go if we don't interfere with them. We are the space in which feelings appear and inhabit.

Ask yourself – do I beat my own heart or does it simply beat itself without any effort on my part?

Ask yourself – am I my hair?

We assume that this is my hair. Do you grow it or does growing of hair simply happen without you having to do anything? Try to stop your hair growing right now.

Ask yourself – did I ask for this colour hair?

These simple exercises can undermine our assumptions about who we think we are.

There is not a little person inside our heads running and directing life, and to whom life is happening. All that is happening is life and then the belief on top of that is that I'm living it, I'm doing it.

Notice what is the 'I' that is asking the question.

AND FINALLY...COMPASSION

◆

As we practise meditation, our seemingly solid sense of self starts to dissolve, revealing our deeper nature, which is one of happiness, love and compassion. As the walls of separation continue to diminish through intelligent meditation, compassion arises to fill the void, bringing us deep satisfaction.

ALTHOUGH WE COME TO MEDITATION and the spiritual life for personal reasons, we may soon come to realize that it is not only ourselves who benefit from it. Our practice of meditation turns out to benefit everybody we come into contact with. When we begin practice, we tend to feel rather cut off and separate from other people; this leaves us feeling as if there is something missing in our lives. Even in our intimate relationships we still feel that we are here inside this body and the world is 'out there'. This sense of unhappy separateness is the human condition and is actually the underlying reason we seek out meditation.

A Universal Quality

What we come to recognize as we practise meditation and our understanding matures is that our deeper nature does not belong exclusively to us, but is universally shared by all living beings. We see that everything and every person is a unique expression of this underlying nature or knowing presence. When this is experienced, we realize that we cannot intentionally hurt anything or anybody again, because we would be hurting our very own self. This experience of compassion is what each of us is knowingly or unknowingly looking for. It is the heart's greatest desire and nothing will satisfy it until it opens and welcomes the whole world and sees and feels everything in it as an experience of its very own self.

The Same, but Different

From this point, life is very much the same and very different. It is the same because outwardly not much may change. We carry on with our ordinary lives, going to work, bringing up the children, washing the dishes, enjoying our friends.

Inwardly everything changes. No longer is there any internal struggle. No longer is everything referenced back to this contracted sense of 'me'. Even though we take wonderful care of ourselves, we realize we are no longer the centre of the universe, and what a relief it is! Where previously we found the world a threatening place, we now trust deeply in the goodness of it. We are no longer frightened; we are free and happy to be nobody.

Patience & Perseverance

This is the fruit of our months and years of practice. These months and years are not without difficulty, however. Time and again we may feel like giving up. Time and again we may feel as if all this work is just not worth the effort. But if we continue we are not disappointed. We will need patience, perseverance and support.

One of the wonderful things I found was meeting up with people who shared a similar vision. It is very important for most of us on this journey to find friends who can support and encourage us and whom we can help in the same way. So you may want to look for a group with whom you feel comfortable. My group meets once a week for meditation and discussion. There will be times when you are feeling confused and you doubt the whole thing; it is then that you may need encouragement and clarity from someone who has been through it themselves. If you cannot find a local group, there are many online groups that you may find helpful. Failing that, you may have to rely on a few good books and your own wisdom and courage.

Be Kind

Though I am encouraging you to sit no matter how you feel, do not bully yourself. Be kind to yourself. If you wonder what that actually means, then find out for yourself. Ask yourself deeply, 'What does it mean to be kind to myself?' Don't look for a quick and neat conceptual response, but allow yourself to be unsure, and if you can do this then at some point you will begin to get a sense of what kindness means in your own experience. This is learning to trust yourself.

What is compassion? It is not merely a sense of sympathy or caring for the person suffering, not simply a warmth of heart towards the person before you, or a sharp clarity of recognition of their needs and pain, it is a sustained and practical determination to do whatever is possible and necessary to help alleviate their suffering.

FROM 'GLIMPSE AFTER GLIMPSE' BY SOGYAL RINPOCHE
RIDER, 1995

AWARENESS PRACTICE

ON COMPASSION

❋

This is a meditation on loving kindness.

Take up your meditation posture and feel your breath for a few minutes. When you feel ready, take your attention to your heart area (middle of the chest) and notice how it feels there. Be honest. Whether you find sadness, happiness, a heavy kind of feeling or virtually nothing, acknowledge it and gently stay with it. You are now ready to move into the five stages of the loving-kindness practice.

1. While staying in your heart area, drop in the phrase, 'May I be happy, may I be well.' Notice any responses you have to these words. Just as in other meditation practices, if you find yourself drifting, then gently and kindly bring yourself back to the present and go back to your heart area. Remember, this is a loving-kindness meditation, and we develop kindness by how we are towards ourselves, so notice if you are critical of yourself, and if you are let the thoughts go and gently come back to your heart area. After a minute or two, drop in the phrase again and rest in the heart. Nothing needs to happen here, you are not looking for a big explosive cosmic love feeling. It is more like you are planting seeds of loving kindness that will grow over time. Do each stage for three to four minutes, then go back to your breath for a minute or two.

2. When it feels right, bring to mind a good friend and wish them well in the same way – 'May you be happy, may you be well.' Again, gently stay in the heart area and be honest about what is there. There may be feelings of warmth, or you may feel pretty neutral or even have feelings of ill will towards your friend. Be absolutely honest about how you feel towards them; honesty also includes not being sure. Sometimes we see that our feelings towards our good friend are mixed, or we realize that we are a little resentful of something they said. All this is absolutely fine and is part of the practice. If you do find warmth and good feelings towards them, then enjoy them and allow them to grow. Do not force any feelings out of awareness and do not try to bring feelings into it. What is happening should be happening because it is happening. After a minute or two, drop in the words again. After three to four minutes allow your friend to stand to one side in your imagination and come back to your breath.

3. Bring to mind a neutral person. This is maybe the post person, or a local shopkeeper. It is someone whom you see about, but you don't have a relationship with. Start in the same way as previous stages, then drop in the phrase once again, and be honest, it is the key. No matter how you feel towards them, it's OK. You may feel very little, but that is fine. It may be worth reflecting that this person wants to be happy just like you. They have fears, they have wishes for a good life just like you. They have people they love and people they find difficult in their life. After three to four minutes, allow this person to stand to one side and come back to the breath.

4. When you feel ready, bring to mind a difficult person – maybe a long-time difficult person, or somebody you are having difficulty with at present. Repeat the practice of the previous stages, then when the time is up allow the difficult person to stand aside and come back to the breath.

5. In the final stage you bring together in your mind all four people from the previous stages. You wish all four people well. You don't need vivid pictures in your mind or to feel each person's presence, it is the intention that matters. Then you include in your awareness all living beings, in an ever-increasing circle. You may casually bring to mind all neighbours in your street or village. Then move out to wish happiness to all people in your country. Again it doesn't matter how you do this; you are certainly not trying to visualize everyone, that would give you quite a headache. It's more about having a sense of people. Then in your own way you can bring other nations to mind. Remember, you don't need to feel something special here; honesty and staying with how you feel is what is important. You can also bring to mind all animals, as they wish to be free from suffering too. After a few minutes of this you can end and spend a few minutes with yourself.

Developing your Loving-Kindness Awareness

I suggest you don't overstretch yourself with this practice as it can be quite demanding. If you decide to practise this a couple of times per week, I suggest you spend a few weeks or even a few months on the first and maybe the second stage too. Don't rush forward with this practice, take your time. When you feel ready, move on to the next stage and then again, moving on to other stages over time. The basis of this practice is the first stage. Get used to wishing yourself well. You are not looking for big breakthroughs with meditation, but a slow, gradual turnaround. If we persevere in this practice, we can start to feel more comfortable with ourselves, our attitude towards ourselves will shift from one that may be based on self-criticism and condemnation to one of warmth and kindness. As we become warm and kind towards ourselves, we naturally become warmer towards others. Kindness always moves to include others in its sphere, but without leaving ourselves out of the picture, so that we become life-centred. What starts to become important is what is best for all concerned, rather than just ourselves or just other people.

You are not looking for big breakthroughs with meditation, but a slow, gradual turnaround.

Coming back to the breath allows us to give ourselves space to see what is happening in the bigger picture. For example, we may find that we have been tense while practising. Coming back to the breath allows us to see yet again how we may be trying to achieve something or trying to make something happen in the practice.

So be kind to yourself here. It's ironic that often we approach the loving-kindness practice with very little kindness, often judging ourselves for falling short of how we think we should be practising.

Be kind, be patient, and enjoy getting to know yourself.

*This is my simple religion.
There is no need for temples; no
need for complicated philosophy.
Our own brain, our own heart is
our temple; the philosophy
is kindness.*

Dalai Lama

Afterword: People on my retreats and courses often ask how to carry on the work when the course is finished, and it is similar with this book. I encourage all to continue their own practice of meditation every day if possible, but without bullying themselves into it. One of the most important things to remember when practising mindfulness meditation is that we are not trying to gain anything. This is because we do not lack anything. We are complete just as we are, though we may not feel that way; it is our deeply held views to the contrary that make us feel incomplete.

Mindfulness is a practice of observing and experiencing the moment. One of the biggest obstacles to it is something I call greed for growth. If possible, forget about results and just do the practice, and the results will come in their own good time. Remember happiness is what we are, unhappiness is what we do. It's less about striving for happiness and more about knowing how we make ourselves unhappy.

I suggest you find a local group with a good meditation teacher, if possible, or at least a group of people who are sympathetic to your aspirations. One such group, which I have been impressed with, is Action for Happiness – www.actionforhappiness.org – a growing worldwide movement for a happier society, founded by Richard Layard. You may find an Action for Happiness group in your area. They provide a forum for each of us to reassess the values by which we live and an opportunity for awareness and change with like-minded people.

As a friend once said to me, 'No matter what your shortcomings are, criticising and condemning yourself never leads to change. All it does is to make you more miserable and feeling hopeless. See the criticism, drop it and cheerfulness will blossom.'

HAPPINESS AND HOW IT HAPPENS

FURTHER RESOURCES

◆

Books

CHARLOTTE JOKO BECK
Nothing Special: Living Zen (HarperCollins, 1993, New York)
Everyday Zen (HarperCollins, 1989, New York)

PEMA CHODRON
The Wisdom of No Escape (Element, 2005, UK)

CHERI HUBER
Sweet Zen (Present Perfect Books, 2000, North Carolina)

JACK KORNFIELD
A Path with Heart (Bantam Books, 1993, New York)

RICHARD LAYARD
Happiness – Lessons from a New Science (Penguin, 2005, USA)

ANTHONY DE MELLO
Awareness (Fount Paperbacks, 1990, UK)

THICH NHAT HANH
The Miracle of Mindfulness (Rider, 1991, London)
Happiness – Essential Mindfulness Practices (Parallax Press, 2009, California)

MATTHIEU RICARD
Happiness – A Guide to Developing Life's Greatest Skill
(Little, Brown & Company, 2006, New York)

AJAHN SUMEDHO
The Sound of Silence (Wisdom Publications, 2007, Massachusetts)

ECKHART TOLLE
The Power of Now (New World Press, 1999, USA)
A New Earth (Dutton, 2005, USA)

JON KABAT ZINN
Wherever You Go, There You Are: Mindfulness Meditation for Everyday Life
(Piatkus Books, 2004, London)

Websites

Action for Happiness – *www.actionforhappiness.org*

Amitavati Retreat Centre (Spain) – *www.amitavati.com*

Dhanakosa – *www.dhanakosa.com*

Gaia House – *www.gaiahouse.co.uk*

Going on Retreat – *www.goingonretreat.com*

Insight Meditation Society – *www.dharma.org*

London Buddhist Centre – *www.lbc.org.uk*

San Francisco Buddhist Center – *www.sfbuddhistcenter.org*

Scott Kiloby – Living realization – *www.kiloby.com*

Shambala Meditation Center (New York) – *www.ny.shambhala.org*

Vajraloka – *www.vajraloka.org*

Wildmind – *www.wildmind.org*

Teachers' websites

ADYASHANTI – *www.adyashanti.org*

EZRA BAYDA & ELIZABETH HAMILTON – *www.zencentersandiego.org*

CHERI HUBER – *www.cherihuber.com*

AJAHN SUMEDHO – *www.amaravati.org*

ECKHART TOLLE – *www.eckharttolle.com*

INDEX

acceptance 36–7, 68–71
addiction 58–9, 72, 95
anger 6, 27, 34, 40, 53, 59, 69, 79, 108–9, 110
anxiety 36, 37, 82, 89, 101–2, 110, 111, 122
awareness 54, 55, 56, 57, 58, 59, 92, 97, 99–100
  meditation and 13, 34, 38
  Pure Awareness 29, 30, 39, 40–1, 70–1
  purpose 13
  trusting in 72–5
awareness practice 6, 7, 98
  acceptance 71
  being present 15
  being still 23
  blaming 111
  compassion 134–8
  desire 103
  emotions 67
  fear 86
  letting go 124
  loneliness 94
  self-identity 129–30
  space between thoughts 119
  thoughts 18
  worry 106

Bayda, Ezra 63, 100
Beck, Charlotte Joko 19, 47
blaming 107–11, 119
body awareness 28, 35, 36–7, 46, 59, 60–7, 129
  anger and 109
  fear and 37, 80, 82–4

letting go 121–2
  loneliness and 92
boredom 93
breath 32–3, 35, 36, 42
Buddha, the 13, 73, 115
busyness 101

change 52–9, 73–4, 107–8, 118–19
chanting 33
compassion 12, 13, 30, 130–8
completeness 20–1, 23
contentment 21, 101–2
curiosity 35, 37–8, 67, 101

Dalai Lama 138
desire 21, 27, 58–9, 95–103
dignity 42

ego 12, 49, 55, 56, 72, 119, 122
egoic agenda 11, 12, 13, 72
egoic mind 18, 23, 30, 56

fear 6, 34, 44, 53, 69, 79–87, 109, 110, 111, 122
  body awareness 37, 80, 82–4
feelings see emotions
freedom 6, 7, 39, 55, 71, 72, 81, 119

genetics 81

'I have enough' 102
intellect 73
Irving, Washington 52

joy of being 97
judging 54, 91, 112, 117, 118, 119

knowing 74

labels 93, 128
letting go 120–4
little me 56, 72, 90–1
loneliness 87–94
loving kindness 134–8
Low, James 105

materialism 95, 99, 100–1, 102
  spiritual 11–12
meditation 11, 12, 25–49, 83,
  115, 116
  awareness and 13, 34, 38
  being present 35–6
  essence 30
  happiness and 48–9
  posture 31–2
mind chatter 40, 123
mindfulness 61, 91, 97, 99, 101–2
mindfulness meditation 6, 7, 98
money 98–9, 100

natural goodness 42–5
no-self 29, 30

panic attacks 84–5
Parsons, Tony 98
Pascal, Blaise 22
peace 21, 49, 61, 119
play 71
present moment 15, 36, 72, 98
prison cell 60
Pure Awareness 29, 30, 39, 40–1,
  70–1
purification 84

relaxation 56–7, 67, 120
repression 68
Rinpoche, Sogyal 133
Rumi 78

Sangharakshita 14, 123
self 13, 30, 46, 56, 88, 114–19
self-acceptance 68–71
self-criticism 57, 137
self-identity 125–30
self-love 43–4, 53
shame 44
simplicity 19–23
sitting in the middle 37
spiritual materialism 11–12
stillness 22, 23

tension 21–2, 35, 37, 63, 66, 70
thoughts 15–18, 21, 30, 40, 46,
  59, 65–6, 127
  fear and 81–6
  space between 119
Tolle, Eckhart 36, 125
Tolstoy, Leo 44–5
Twain, Mark 122
two arrows 75

Walcott, Derek 38
Wilde, Oscar 17
wisdom 12, 13, 15, 30, 47, 73,
  81, 83, 90
witnessing/watching 28–9, 35, 39,
  53–4, 56, 69, 120–1, 124
worry 46, 104–6

DEDICATION & ACKNOWLEDGEMENTS

I would like to dedicate this book to my Mum and Dad, thank you for everything.

'No man is an island entire of itself,' wrote John Donne, and it is the same with this book. It is the result of experience gained from many sources and I am grateful to all.

I want to thank all those who have inspired and helped in the writing of this book. I would like to thank my teacher, Sangharakshita, for introducing me to Buddhism and meditation. He showed there was a way to live life with richness, depth and meaning. I am forever grateful.

I would like to thank the enthusiastic and delightful Monica Perdoni, the commissioning editor for Ivy Press, who had the perceptiveness to contact me out of the blue and ask me to write this book.

I would like to acknowledge Jayne Ansell, senior editor at Ivy Press, who showed nothing but patience and kindness in the face of my sometimes imprecise and vague way of going about things, and Jenni Davis, my copy editor, who always kept things light with her delightful humour and whose brilliance shines on every page of this book.

Many thanks to Sharon McKee, who was the first person to take this work seriously and gave me the confidence to carry on.

Thank you to Dylan McKee, the young technical genius, for his help in moments of panic.

And last but certainly not least, a huge thank you to my loving partner Gaynor, who believed in me when I didn't and who has supported and encouraged me every step of the way.